Understanding the Human Mind

The Powerful Force of Imagination

Jason Browne

© Copyright 2020 - All rights reserved.

The content contained within this book may not be reproduced, duplicated or transmitted without direct written permission from the author or the publisher.

Under no circumstances will any blame or legal responsibility be held against the publisher, or author, for any damages, reparation, or monetary loss due to the information contained within this book, either directly or indirectly.

Legal Notice:

This book is copyright protected. It is only for personal use. You cannot amend, distribute, sell, use, quote or paraphrase any part, or the content within this book, without the consent of the author or publisher.

Disclaimer Notice:

Please note the information contained within this document is for educational and entertainment purposes only. All effort has been executed to present accurate, up to date, reliable, complete information. No warranties of any kind are declared or implied. Readers acknowledge that the author is not engaged in the rendering of legal, financial, medical or professional advice. The content within this book has been derived from various sources. Please consult a licensed professional before attempting any techniques outlined in this book.

By reading this document, the reader agrees that under no circumstances is the author responsible for any losses, direct or indirect, that are incurred as a result of the use of the information contained within this document, including, but not limited to, errors, omissions, or inaccuracies.

Table of Contents

INTRODUCTION 1

CHAPTER 1: WHAT IS REALITY? 7
- RELIGIOUS CONCLUSIONS 7
- SCIENTIFIC FRAGMENTATION 12
- PHILOSOPHICAL REALITY 17
- THE GREATEST MINDS 19

CHAPTER 2: THE CONSCIOUS VERSUS THE SUBCONSCIOUS .. 25
- THE ICEBERG HIERARCHY 25
- THE SUBCONSCIOUS PLAYING FIELD 29
- ACTIVATING THE SUBCONSCIOUS MIND 34

CHAPTER 3: IMAGINATION IS THE KEY 41
- WRITING YOUR STORY 41
- FUNCTIONAL INFLUENCE 45
- UNLOCKING THE BEST VERSION OF YOU 51

CHAPTER 4: THE NEUROSCIENCE BEHIND IT 57
- MICROSCOPIC CREATIVITY 57
- THOUGHTFUL CONTROL 63
- MANIPULATING REALITY 68

CHAPTER 5: WATCH YOUR INNER MONOLOGUE 73
- TAPPING INTO THE WRONG WELL 74
- THE ARCHITECT'S AWARENESS 79
- DESIGNING THE NEW BLUEPRINT 83

CHAPTER 6: PRIMING THE SUBCONSCIOUS MIND FOR SUCCESS 89
- CHOOSING YOUR DESTINATION 89

Creative Journaling 94
Designing Your Vision Board 97
The Power of Meditation 99
The Essence of Creative Visualization 101
A Short Stroll 105

CONCLUSION **109**

REFERENCES **113**

Shakti Gawain once said: "Every moment of your life is infinitely creative and the universe is endlessly bountiful. Just put forth a clear enough request, and everything your heart truly desires must come to you."

Introduction

The world has endless possibilities, but so does your human mind. You've always wondered why other people find success, revel in unshakable relationships, and increase their wealth. It may seem unfair that life is filled with opportunities that aren't in your hands. You're not sure if you should admire the people who create unimaginable lives for themselves, or if you should envy them with a pinch of salt. You have all these questions about how someone can build an empire from nothing.

What about the person who came from a poor background, stood up to seemingly insurmountable challenges, and walked away without a bruise? Maybe you struggle to understand why some people never give up and keep pursuing goals that seem unreachable. Are they arrogant or do they unwittingly have too much confidence is something that seems impossible? Many people have come to know that the human mind is the source of all possibilities, opportunities, and success.

You might've read other books about the mind that fell short because they didn't give you the insight people need to make the changes. Maybe the information lacked quality and didn't make sense. It hasn't stopped your pursuit of learning how to change your reality, either. It's not so much of a mindset alteration that's needed, but rather harnessing the powers that lie within a framework that existed before you were born.

You probably know about the imagination and have likely practiced a few techniques that were shy of mastering it. It's also become common knowledge that the mind is split into two partitions that have disadvantages and advantages unless they're brought together. How does one do this, though? Your current knowledge doesn't sustain the evidence to prove the power of both consciousnesses.

You don't know how to pull them together in a streamlined function. Imagination has more to do with connecting these two partitions than most people know. The people who know about it and use its benefits are those you envy or admire. They've researched and learned about the science, philosophy, neurology, and spirituality that synchronizes everything in the mind.

They've used their powers to create a life that makes other people wonder what they did wrong. There's an inconceivable fallacy surrounding the imagination. People become afraid of judgment if they use it accordingly, even though science agrees on how we can master it to open opportunities that weren't there before. It's mentioned in childhood literature and often used to stimulate kids' minds in movies and games.

This explains the fears; because who wants to use childish endeavors to form a success story in adulthood? It's simple, we'd have to agree that kids harness a power that adults neglect. However, the truth is far more complex and one must understand the human mind to see how creativity can cause an explosion of satisfaction in relationships, work, business, home, and talents. There's nothing childish about such a powerful tool.

How can we argue with those who've created boundless wealth and reputations that exceed fairy tales? Jim Carey's a beloved celebrity who's gained wealth beyond his dreams, and you guessed it, he uses his imagination to do it (Williams, 2015). He wasn't alone because even Arnold Schwarzenegger built his body stature by using his imaginative tool. Will Smith gained his success by believing that we attract the life we want with our imagination.

He wrote his dreams on paper and said that it shall come true. That paper was a check for millions of dollars that he committed to earning before he became the face we know today. Smith was a struggling actor who walked with an imagined figure in his pocket for a decade. However, his unwavering faith in his imagination was what turned that check into reality. Newspapers have been sharing stories about how athletes use the imagination to bring home the success stories they do.

The New York Times exposed how Canadian bobsledder Lyndon Rush used his imagination to map his route on the treacherous course for optimal results (Clarey, 2014). Olympic teams from France even brought sports psychologists along to the Russian games to help participants use this masterful skill to win. The power of the human mind isn't only seen in successful people either. It's led to scientific research into understanding why the imagination is so influential.

I share many of the theories and experiments in this book to make sure you use the tool correctly. It can also be used improperly and this causes more harm than good. The imagination allows us to see the unseen truths about what is needed. Science cannot exist without it. Not only can science confirm how we can empower the human mind to fully expand our horizons, but it's also used to teach people to become engineers, scientists, and inventors (Vavra et al., 2011).

Do you think an inventor could build their product without using the imagination? Now, that would be impossible. Being unable to use the imagination is the only impossibility that exists. The secret to using it lies within science, religious scriptures, and philosophy combined. That's where I fell short on my journey to optimize my future in the beginning.

I relied heavily on one or the other, not realizing that using all the information we have available to us is the way I'd master this skill. Being on the ranch allows me time to research, experiment, and apply the techniques to my life. I can attune to nature, family, success, and the reality I choose to create. I've spent 20 years getting to where and who I am today. My fascination with the mind opened my opportunities to design the life I want. I have days when my mind is flooded with information and I accept this.

I welcome epiphanies into my reality and use them to my advantage. My mental exercises have brought me to a point where I can achieve anything that I set my mind to. The world became my oyster and I had no option but to start putting my knowledge on paper. I had to share it with you because positivity isn't easily contained. This book focuses on the imagination because it can open doors you never knew existed. It puts an end to the debates between the Big Bang Theory and the incredible prophets who once walked this earth.

God and science have never been in agreement about what reality is, until I puzzled it together. The void between the conscious and subconscious minds might seem great, but it's far simpler to connect them with our imagination. I had to research neuroscience in my free time to understand how the consciousnesses impact each other. Nonetheless, I found the key to unlocking the secrets and forming a reality I desire. The human mind is far more fascinating when you probe it.

Consensus theories give us credence to follow the simple techniques that could turn our boring, bland, and unsuccessful lives into something we dreamed of as children. You'll learn all about the proven-techniques that allow you to communicate with the auspicious subconscious mind and how to attract the positive future you deserve. Your habits will change to suit your new reality and you'll welcome the changes when you see how enjoyable the exercises are.

I might cover technical details, but you'll understand it and apply the solutions without struggle. The exercises will prime your subconscious mind for optimal results and you'll become the driver of your mental vehicle. Many exercises can be customized to your needs and desires. There are seven rules by which you should practice them and you won't believe how they can be simple and powerful at the same time. A framework has been set in place for you and all you need to do is to take charge of the new routines.

It will come naturally to you once the brain has been trained with the help of science. You'll no longer attract negative outcomes with faulty control over the mind. You won't fall prey to expressing how you knew things would happen this way again unless it's what you wanted. Use your mind to manifest the desires your heart longs for, and get the partner you want, the career you choose, and the life that makes others envy you.

All you must bring to the table is a bountiful sense of curiosity and the attention span of the genius that resides deep within your mind. Allow your eagerness and energy to open your mind to unspeakable changes by continuing your curiosity.

Chapter 1:

What is Reality?

Does a falling tree in a deserted forest make a noise as it crashes against the ground? This question has often been used to establish an understanding of reality because was the noise real if no one heard it? Understandably, the question about what reality is cannot reach a unanimous conclusion. We start our journey by learning about various opinions within this field of thought while addressing the nuances of each. You'll quickly realize that many commonalities are more profound than the variances and this ultimately designs our 'truth.'

Religious Conclusions

Religion is hogwash to some people, but it's a reality to its followers. Christianity is one of the oldest religions, as written by Paul the Apostle a few millennia back. Unbelievers see the Bible as an instruction manual on how to live our lives. They don't realize that Christianity goes much deeper than that. It also teaches its followers about what their purpose is, the beauty of

God's creation, and the spiraling destruction of evil. The Bible intends to teach people about liberation and the healing work of Jesus Christ. We also learn to respect history and find the nature of wisdom and truth. The Christian God encumbers everything, created all, and lives presently in everyone who accepts him.

Therefore, a part of God is within every person, almost like we are part of his celestial body. Followers believe that we're God's breath. Christians have their idea of reality as everything God willed and created. This means that Christians ultimately need to believe in something they can't see. Their reality is both tangible in the physical creation in front of them and non-tangible in the promise of another unseen reality in heaven or hell when they leave this world. The reality behind Christianity is scrutinized because it requires people to believe in God's creation and will.

However, the Bible says that man has free will. That's a slight contradiction on one hand, and understandable on another. It means that free will gives them endless possibilities originally provided by God's will. Christianity and science haven't seen eye to eye since the latter takes a tangible view on reality. Science has exploded into fragments of proving what reality is and how it forms. The Big Bang Theory has pushed aside religious notions which became secularized from the sciences. The truth is that every science is fragmented from another and none of them agree with each other. Still, people became attuned to believe in what can be proven.

However, many scientists describe the consciousness as a soul, but isn't this precisely what Christianity teaches? The soul is mentioned numerous times in the Bible. God's will is a reality to Christians, but they also believe that God will change their reality as they connect to him soulfully. Christians are taught to live by the principles of the Bible, and they can ask him in prayer for what they need to be changed in their reality. Christianity isn't the only religion that teaches us about the soul. Many religions teach similar principles and others believe in reincarnation. The biggest similarity among them is that there's a divine being that maintains the universe and that life continues in some form after death.

The Prophet Muhammed brought us Islamic beliefs. He wrote his own book of instructions instead of giving this major responsibility to an apostle. The Quran also teaches Islamists to either follow a life that leads to damnation or eternal bliss. They also have a counter-argument for science. Nonbelievers use grandeur materialism but do they have any proof that this is their only reality? Science cannot prove that tangible objects alone are reality or that nothing exists after. Islamists see materialization as a superficial fallacy because possessions don't exist in the next life. Science disagrees with faith though because it tries to prove tangibility. Therefore, these two sectors also disagree, even though their ideations are similar, as you'll learn soon.

Ancient scriptures are often scrutinized; however, history shows a tangible trace of Prophet Muhammed's existence. The facts of his life were carefully preserved and cannot be contested through science. The Prophet warned of a damning future where reality is all we have. He taught us that it's unchangeable if we don't carefully choose the life we want after death. Compare this to the weather channel warning you about a natural disaster. A hurricane is on its way and you have a decision to make. You can either evacuate or believe that the experts are wrong. The reality taught by Prophet Muhammed is simple. It's something we can't physically see, but we must believe that our soul will go either way when we die.

Hinduism is another ancient religion that often collides with science. Hindus believe in a trinity God where Brahman is the main deity. At a time that isn't clear in scriptures, a vast ocean flooded over the universe, and Vishnu washed up on a serpent. A lotus flower formed in his navel and when he awoke, he told Brahman that it was time to create the world. The lotus had three leaves. The first leaf created the heavens, the second painted the skies, and the third formed the earth before Brahman populated it with life forms. Shiva is believed to be the third God, and he destroys the earth with fire. This starts the cycle again and Brahman awaits the waters to create the world once more.

Hindus believe that the world, soul, and reality exist in loops and call this *samsara*. Hinduism is far more complex though because every God is believed to be a segment of Brahman. Vishnu is the preserver deity of Brahman and his wife is called Lakshmi. The female persona of Brahman is one of the millions they have, but she's in charge of maintaining the loop according to people's *dharma*. Dharma is the Hindu word for truth or reality, and it's influenced by the way people portray themselves. Their behavior or social order will determine their hierarchy and presence in the next loop. Dharma can also be understood as to how we must live our lives to be favored upon in the next life.

The interesting factor in Hinduism is that no manifestation of the original God is any less than the great deity himself. Worshiping or following the guidance of any of these Gods is living by Brahman's truth. The term Brahman is similar to God in Christianity. These Gods are everything, reside in everyone, and manifest in every animal.

Followers choose their God based on personality traits as well. Lakshmi is thought to bring good fortune and grace, whereas Kali is often seen as a figure with flaming eyes. All these Gods look different and vary in persona, but they still make up part of Brahman. Now we have an important lesson to learn from Hinduism. They believe in a term called *Maya*. This means that the world we see in front of us is an illusion of manifestations of the Gods and materialistic objects.

Yes, we have bodies, personalities, and thoughts, but our reality projects into these formations. Hindus believe that the loop is reality, but the Maya effect changes our reality prospectively. Kali is perceived as a monster with her flaming eyes, but she's a protector and nurturing, motherly Goddess. This projected reality is also how we interpret ourselves. This is an interesting fact because Hinduism also teaches us that our illusion reality is controlled by the Gods, much like Christianity. God's will creates the illusion of what we see through our beliefs. Even the Prophet Muhammed spoke of a chosen reality that leads down two paths to an eternal reality.

Scientific Fragmentation

Now we need to learn about what science has found in the various fragments of discipline. The first theory of reality comes in the form of quantum physics. These physicists place everything under a microscope. They want to see the connection of molecules made up by even tinier atoms. Atoms were first thought to be the final fragment of everything that exists until scientists found elementary particles that are even tinier. This posed a problem because they were too small to see even with the best microscopes. Scientists believe that reality is only what can be seen and elementary particles made this impossible. The human eye can only see in the light. Try distinguishing something in the dark.

Light bounces off an object and reflects into our retinas to be processed by the brain. This information turns into an image in our minds. You can't see something that your electromagnetic waves in the brain can't actively interact with. Elementary particles are so minuscule that these waves can't touch them even with additional light added. Science has tried to solve this problem by creating shorter wavelengths of light to hit the particle targets. Unfortunately, this creates larger energy around the wave and this changes the particles when they interact. In this sense, our interactions with these particles change their formations. Human beings can't currently interact with particles unless they change them and this is called the Heisenberg Uncertainty Principle.

This principle is the basis of every quantum physics development and why various scientific disciplines contest each other. The truth is that no one knows what a particle looks like, but we know of their existence. A new method was needed to understand particles. It was suggested that a particle is a spatial point in the universe because everything is made up of particles. Scientists did what anyone would and used mathematics to examine these tiny fragments of reality better. This is how *M-Theory* was born. The point particles are also called electrons, which each have a mass and charge that create a force. Now scientists could try to measure the mass and energy because no particle is identical to another one.

They are unique and this is why no comparisons of deoxyribonucleic acid (DNA) match 100%. Our DNA are clusters of particles that form molecules. Nevertheless, the measurements is how Quantum Field Theory was discovered. Particles are either quarks, leptons, or bosons depending on their mathematical measurements. This science helps us devise an image of what the universe looks like.

However, mathematics doesn't solve every problem. The Theory of Relativity focuses on gravitational particles because their structure is different. A weak force is made of the particles in quantum physics, a stronger particle is called a photon, and the strongest force is made of gluon particles. Their energy and mass are different, creating a larger force.

However, gravitational forces need to be perfectly measurable, which wasn't mathematically possible yet. That's why quantum physics and gravity don't make sense together. We cannot perfectly measure the distance between the particles. Physicists tried to invent new gravity particles that could be added to the regular ones but this failed miserably. They didn't stop trying though because the marriage of gravity and quantum physics would give us an exact idea of reality. String Theory was introduced to rather measure a collection or string of particles and the unique energy they vibrate. Different particles strung together give scientists something more measurable and even includes gravity particles.

The biggest problem with String Theory is that it can't be measured in a single strain. It requires 10 dimensions or the theory falls apart. String Theory is currently like trying to build a train without an engine. The math is correct now, but we cannot see or interact with the other dimensions we need yet.

String Theory and Quantum Gravity teach us that the universe is made up of energy-matter, but they still can't measure time or space. These theories have simply given us an idea of infinity. That's why the universe is infinite because it's vastly misunderstood. We cannot say what matter or mathematical forces are outside of our current advancements. The universe consists of infinite consciousnesses and life forms created by delicate collisions between the existing forces.

We can also only measure spatial dimensions and not time. We know that time exists but it perceivably moves forward alone, whereas particles can move forwards, backward, sideways, and up or down. This makes the space-time continuum another mystery.

Some scientists wonder whether matter truly exists or if time is merely an illusion. So, how do we turn something invisible into reality if our light waves are incapable of seeing these particles? How do we understand reality if the science surrounding it is theoretical? This is where consciousness plays a role because it's how we perceive the information we see that determines our current reality and even science can't disagree with this fact.

Photons are the particles our consciousness uses presently in light. They're stronger than quantum particles and have been studied under different conditions. Photons don't react singly or logically. They simply create an image. Physicist Thomas Young experimented on the behavior of photons when the light was directed into a double-slit barrier (Ananthaswamy, 2018). It was originally thought that the photons would go through one slit and pile up behind it. The more obvious result was that photons divided and spread variant light through the different slits. The photons also started collapsing once they got through the barrier.

This is simple to understand if you shine a light through a wall of holes. The light concentrates through the holes and shines on the other side of the wall; however, it becomes weaker as it travels further. Furthermore, the larger concentration of light moving through the holes also weakens and the photons collapse faster in the distance. It might've been hard to measure photon particles in the dark ages, but measuring light has become possible, even at home now. The reason these theories are important is that photons are the particles that help us see the reality formed by other particles. That's why the universe has been established scientifically as a multiverse, because even scientists can't comprehend what lies beyond their photonic view.

Therefore, science might believe that reality is what tangibly exists, but this can't be true. Reality is only what the photonic imagery in our conscious minds can distinguish. It doesn't mean that nothing else exists. No one can say the tree fell silently if they weren't there to prove it. The person who witnessed the tree's demise photonically, or was close enough to hear it, is the person whose reality says that it made a crushing noise.

Philosophical Reality

Plato is a popular name in Athenian philosophy, and he believed that reality isn't experienced through the senses alone (Pigliucci, 2020). Sensory phenomena aren't strong enough and couldn't predict the true essence of reality. The senses aren't trustworthy because they can be influenced externally. We need intellect to process the sensory information as well. The reality we see when we look at a table is conceptual. Using our conscious intellect is how we translate the concept to universal perceptions. Plato suggested that we must increase our intellect so that we can investigate the true nature behind objects.

Ancient stoicism is where we believe that objects in existence are the true meaning of reality, similar to science. You've learned about how particles can't be seen and this proves that we can't rely solely on materialism. This theory also can't explain why everything looks different. We can't say that a chair and a table look the same. Even String Theory teaches us that every string of energy resonates with unique particles. Nevertheless, Stoics called the singular particles *pneuma* and this 'breath' has four substrates. The first is the singular fragment that exists in an object. The second is the cohesion of the pneuma to give an object a collective form.

The third is the soul which gives us movement and power over cohesive collections. The fourth is called logos and this is the logic we find in what we see. However, humans are the only beings who have all four because rocks don't have logos or soul. Stoics and scientists can agree that all matter is made of something, whether it's particles or breath. Plato is the man who disagreed with this monist and materialistic view. He said that matter couldn't always be physical if concepts were included. The soul is our consciousness in the scientific realm, but it doesn't have a measurable or tangible shape or form.

We need to consciously conceptualize information before it becomes true. This means that reality can't only be based on what exists. Yes, something must exist to be real, but does that mean thoughts aren't real? The Stoics believed that the soul is physical, yet, scientists haven't been able to pinpoint it. They can find the conscious minds which think, feel, and decide how to react to sensory stimuli, but there's no precise location other than the brain. Scrutinizers would either have to admit that concepts don't exist or that they're made of matter in the brain. Time is a concept, but does it exist? Plato's theory suggests that we must believe that concepts are existing or time is just an illusion.

That's where Athenian philosophy changed because existence can be two things. A chair might exist physically, but a thought subsists beyond where the naked eye can see. It's a substrate of matter in the consciousness. Time doesn't exist according to this data, but it does subsist. It's causation of matter that exists. You can think about negotiating a better deal with someone, but only your physical body can do so.

Everything we see is merely a hallucination of what our subsisting consciousness translates, but concepts require the existing matter to materialize into visual effects. The brain is existing and the conscious mind subsists.

The Greatest Minds

How does this help us understand reality better? Quantum physics tries to teach us that space and time must be a linear reality. Albert Einstein was the masterful scientist who broke the static theory with his relativity theory (Fortune Magazine, 1994). His popular formula suggests that the result of energy released from particles must be measured by the mass and speed of light or charge squared. Light intervenes with particles and this comes from our conscious examination of an object. The photon speed is constant and can change the matter. Gravity or gluons can also influence the form of the matter. Gravity being the strongest form of a particle means that it can even alter light or photons.

The Chaos Theory finally trumped the relativity and static theories. Previous theories suggested that matter isn't very malleable because photons and gluons don't have enough influence. Einstein proved this wrong and the Chaos Theory taught us that reality is changeable. The Chaos Theory and the Hinduism 'Maya' effect sound too similar now. This is why science can never completely ignore ancient theories. Godel's theorem is a higher mathematical strategy that also teaches us that concepts cannot translate to perceptions without the influence of external factors. No one can know everything without investigating external factors and that's how Plato's intelligence theory helps us.

Aristotle was Plato's student who had his own ideas about reality. He turned it into a tangible concept again (Bartleby Research, 2020). However, the secret to Aristotle's idea was that reality cannot exist, tangible or not, without the mind processing the information it captures through the senses. He explained that truth is only in the eye of the beholder at a precise time, because the brain processes the external, sensory information available at that moment. Reality in his terms can also be understood as the process between potential and actuality, known as causality. For example, if you seek happiness, then finding it will fulfill a potential you had in mind. Our reality will change form as we consciously make decisions to reach the potential of what we desire.

Our minds eventually store the concepts of our reality and this can also be seen in physical existence. You'll always know that a table has legs once you've conceptualized this enough. Then we have the famous Buddhist teachings as well. Did you know that free will, as given by the Christian God, is the same thing as mindfulness? This means that all religions have free will with the hope of reward at the end of this worldly existence. Buddhists believe in consciousness and how it's influenced internally and externally. It is how we make decisions, but it's also influenced by the beliefs, morals, and desires of the external world. Consciousness is similar to a time particle that cannot be defined as here or there. It can be everywhere at once.

The reason for this is believed through science and philosophy as the concept of time or consciousness being existing for only a millisecond before it moves along (Hahn, 2009). Take a flame-dancer as an example here. The flame isn't static and is constantly moving, creating the effect that the fire is circling the dancer. That's because the particle making it is constantly moving through space. Consciousness is only a flash of reality that exists in the present millisecond you experience it while processing information from your senses at the same time. Every movement of a living being on earth is fragmented into milliseconds of reality. Buddhism and science agree that nothing is permanent and that's probably why time can't be interacted with photonically.

The reason mindfulness and free will are the same things is that they both take place in the reality of that millisecond. A decision can only be made in the reality of ever-moving particles. Mindfulness teaches us how to control free will by becoming aware of the exact movement of these processes in the conscious mind. Buddhism also follows the idea of dharma. Their concept of dharma is to seek the eternal goodness that comes after the death of our present form, by speaking, acting, and thinking with good karma. The karma we share with others will ensure a reward for us in the next life we live, whether it's on earth again or in another Buddhist reality.

Reality has been fraught with ideas of materialization, but the concept of millisecond shifts means that even death takes place every time we move into the next phase of reality. The greatest minds in history have shown us that reality isn't what it seems, even in science. Quantum theories have taught us that the energy force that's conceptualized as reality can change as it collides with photons or gravity. It's always changing and this means that religion and philosophy aren't the enemies of perceived truth. Remove yourself from any one of the schools of thought in this chapter and look at the similarities as a whole. Reality isn't stable and changes from moment to moment.

Our interpretation of reality is consciously guiding our perception of these changes. The truth is that nothing in this world is certain. Even evolution has disproved this fallacy. What is certain is that our idea of reality must include the fundamentals of our perceptions of these changes.

So, what is reality? I want you to be open-minded as we move forward in this book. One can generalize the understanding of reality as particles or breath dependent on your inner perceptions. It's wholeheartedly reliant on your interpretations. Reality also isn't genuine until you decide that it's so. The world is grayer than it can ever be black and white. The question then becomes, how we can influence reality if it's this malleable? Influencing it correctly could prove favorable.

Chapter 2:

The Conscious Versus the Subconscious

Have you ever had a brilliant idea spring into your mind at the most unexpected moment? This is instigated by the powerful consciousness that underlines everything about you. You might be familiar with the consciousness that is nearly as complicated as quantum physics, or you might be unaware of the supremacy within your mind. Science remains a complicated subject, until you learn about the great advancements made in the human mind already. The conscious and subconscious minds will be revealed in this chapter so that you can use the full potential of each level.

The Iceberg Hierarchy

Sigmund Freud was an astronomical contender in researching the human mind more than a century ago. He was an Austrian neurologist who targeted the pathology of the psychological mind and how one can repair the inconsistencies within it (Buckley, 2019). His research blew the minds of many other psychotherapists and neurologists, when he designed a hierarchy of the human mind. Freud understood that diseased pathologies reside deep within the mind and the person struggling with these psychological issues wasn't even aware of them. This is where the famous iceberg analogy comes from. Freud figured out that the mind is layered in various levels of consciousness.

He described our consciousness as an iceberg floating in the ocean. The tip of the iceberg was called the conscious level and only pertained to 10% of the mind. The iceberg continued under the ocean where another 90% of the mind resided in two more levels. The first layer under the water was called the preconscious mind. The very tip of the underwater iceberg was called the unconscious mind. This research led to multiple avenues that confirmed what Freud suggested. However, it's important to note that the unconscious mind was later referred to as the subconscious mind. The word unconscious related too much to fainting and being unaware of our surroundings.

Unbeknownst, this is understandably what Freud meant when he named it the unconscious mind but it was often misunderstood due to the name. Freud also explained how the hierarchy worked. The conscious level is where we are aware of thoughts, emotions, behavior, and memories. It's also the logical thinker of the three levels. The conscious mind is what you use every minute of your waking life to think about what the next option is. The memories within the conscious mind aren't permanent either. They reside in the lower levels but can be surfaced for awareness when the conscious mind needs them. The preconscious mind is where all the information exists that can be brought into awareness.

The subconscious level is the deepest part of our minds. It contains the largest memory banks and acts as an internal encyclopedia. This storage area keeps our memories, thoughts, emotions, and beliefs out of our conscious awareness. Our desires also live within the subconscious mind. The reason most of the information is stored here is that it's unpleasant, painful, unacceptable, or it conflicts with our thoughts on the surface. Think about the conscious mind as the one that stirs thoughts of being thirsty. Those thoughts might've surfaced from the preconscious mind because this is what it does. It waits until its thoughts can be brought into awareness.

The subconscious mind can also push unwanted thoughts into the preconscious and then into subliminal awareness. The last time you drank water in this town it tasted like metal. Immediately, you feel hesitant to drink it now. The subconscious mind has influenced your final decision with the desire not to taste metal. This desire was created automatically without rational thought from the unpleasant memories beneath. That's why Freud studied the levels, because the subconscious mind stores information that is crucial to repairing broken minds. Little did he know that his work would open the world to using this hierarchy to their advantage in healthy minds too.

The automatic surfacing was the source of painful and unwanted memories, but the subconscious mind was below logical thoughts and couldn't reason with these ideas. This helps us understand how reality becomes what we decide for it to be. This person's reality is that this town's water is disgusting. The subconscious mind alters our decision without us even knowing about it. Transfer this evidence to a seemingly healthy mind now; the subconscious mind also influences the conscious level when you're trying to think of a possible future where you're pursuing great ambitions. You're hoping for a promotion at work and it stirs thoughts in your conscious level. The subconscious mind will interfere with the processes above, if left to do so automatically.

The subconscious is always active whether you want it to be or not. It doesn't need to rest like the conscious mind, because it's responsible for keeping you alive. It controls your breathing, heart rate, and other vital signs. You don't need to think about breathing, do you? It happens automatically and this is how the subconscious can alter your thoughts about promotion because it controls your desires, whether this is logical or not. The subconscious is where your behavior originates through influence on the conscious mind. It's what makes you human and cannot be ignored when you're pursuing your dreams. It doesn't only contain negative memories but it also holds the key to optimal desires.

Your conscious mind can want and desire all it likes, but if the subconscious mind isn't attuned to the same urges, then you've lost the battle before you began. It cannot think on its own and needs concise information. The best you can do is learn about the subconscious mind before you proceed.

The Subconscious Playing Field

Digging deeper into the subconscious will reveal its power and influence to make you understand the relationship with the conscious level better. The subconscious is much like a loyal servant that's intent is built upon structure and clear communication. It has no sense of humor and can't think for itself. It won't query instructions logically and doesn't even intentionally influence the conscious mind. The subconscious plays a role that's been set, before you even knew it.

The servant does what it's told to do from the conscious mind without searching through the evidence of its vast database. Think about the iceberg again. The bottom tip never sees the surface of the ocean. It has no external factors influencing it other than the conscious mind's perception of what's going on around it.

That's why wires get crossed in the communication between the two. The conscious mind tries to be rational, but the communications can be warped like a broken telephone. The subconscious is much older than the logical processes in your brain. It exists before we're even born and starts collecting information for its database before we learn how to interact with the world, never mind learning logic. Early childhood development can help us understand how the subconscious mind or our beliefs, behavior, and desires are formed before the age of eight (van Rensburg, 2017). Critical thinking only starts forming around eight-years-old. We're navigating blindly with the information stored in the subconscious mind before this.

Everything people say or do around us is stored as evidence and the subconscious mind believes that this is all facts. The adult mind has formed a 'logical' filter that lies between the conscious and subconscious minds, but this was missing in your early childhood. Comparing this to adults can help you understand what's needed. Adults have five different brain waves that constitute and sort information that comes into the conscious mind. Gamma waves travel at more than 40 cycles per second, and are the photons that process higher thinking or cognitive functions in the logical side of the brain. The left brain is thought to be where reason lies and is highly active in adults.

The second wave is called Beta and this one travels at 12 to 40 cycles per second. Beta waves are active when adults are focused intensely on a conversation, while they need to think at the same time. Alpha waves travel between eight and 12 cycles per second. This wave starts bridging the gap between the conscious and subconscious minds by filtering out distractions. Theta waves travel much slower between four and eight cycles per second. Most people will be asleep at this stage where the subconscious mind is more active than the conscious mind. Delta waves travel the slowest between zero and four cycles per second. Delta waves are commonly seen in people who are deeply asleep. The subconscious mind is in control and the conscious thinker rests now. Infants and toddlers run on these slower waves because their brains aren't functioning on higher processes yet.

Consciousness is most influenced during the lower frequencies. The subconscious mind gathers information for the database as the conscious mind sleeps, or is nonexistent in kids yet. This means that your consciousness had eight years of processing irrational information before you could guide it, which explains why the subconscious has developed who you are, your beliefs, your desires, and your automatic responding habits. It has become a framework from which the conscious mind unwittingly collects data. The framework has been developed by our parents and the environment we grew up in, making it rather set in its ways. Decisions become a habit even if they make no sense.

An infant has slow brain waves that only cycle a couple of times per second. Alpha waves only start coming in at age six and the higher consciousness beta waves commonly kick in at age 12. Toddlers rely on their right brain which is thought to focus more on creativity, subjective perspective, imagination, and intuition. Kids are pretty primitive at this stage. Babies are only frightened by loud noises and falling. The other fears start developing as they interact with the world. The subconscious mind identifies and associates experiences with fear, love, and desire to create the framework. The identification of an experience leads to feelings that associate a previous behavior that worked for them. Limiting beliefs are programmed in this stage and can even hold adults back subconsciously in their later years.

Children in this theta wave stage are easily influenced. They believe everything you tell them is factual. Some call this a trance-like state where the subconscious mind collects information and stores it without conscious effort. Let's say that your preschool teacher always told you that you're stupid. This forms a programmable belief in the subconscious mind and when you interview for a position in your twenties, the subconscious automatically and unintentionally regulates your fears about the interview. You start thinking that you're not smart enough to get the position or you just don't have the skills required.

Both consciousnesses have their purposes in the hierarchy too. The conscious mind might take a back seat to the subconscious, but the first one is where your rationale exists. The subconscious mind will use previous experiences from your internalized reality to make decisions without thinking, whereas the conscious mind will use logic to traverse any experiences. The conscious mind also has the advantage of critical thinking to solve problems. It can calculate sensory input to understand what the best outcome will be. The subconscious mind will learn from this processing if it's repeated enough. Learning to solve a budgeting problem is conscious thinking, but it becomes a subconscious habit once you've been budgeting successfully for a long time.

The conscious mind can also appreciate and understand things when the subconscious mind can't. The subconscious relies on the critical thinker to devise solutions and will store the memory when you succeed. Feeding the subconscious with solutions and good experiences will give it other options to automate when required. This is where the subconscious mind's advantage comes into play. It will always look for the shortest and fastest solution known to work. This is a disadvantage if you keep feeding it with negative experiences, because it never questions any input from the conscious mind. It simply follows it like a loyal servant, waiting to obey. It will always manifest what you instruct it to create.

It doesn't think, but rather does, operates, and allows things to be. We learned that reality is what you make it, so allow your subconscious mind to create a new byproduct of your beliefs and experiences. However, you must know that it won't always unfold exactly the way you consciously want it to. You must intelligently activate the brain waves required to instruct your subconscious mind clearly to avoid miscommunications. The good news is that it's possible to recreate the delta, theta, and alpha brain waves required to activate the subconscious mind and give it instructions. Its response will depend on your communication with it.

Activating the Subconscious Mind

The subconscious manifests our desires and ambitions. However, we must dive into the brain waves required to reach it. Our conscious mind runs on the highly focused beta waves because it needs to think. This is where our intelligence, analytical thinking, planning, problem-solving, and critical thoughts act as a mini-processor. It's a superficial essence of our being where self-esteem, self-criticism, and judgment are based on short-term memory. It's the part of your brain that says you aren't good enough to reach the desires you want, because the subconscious mind is influencing it without your knowledge.

The next brain waves take you into the theta and alpha frequencies where longer-term memories and thoughts are hiding. This is what Freud called the preconscious state that divides the conscious and subconscious minds. This is already deeper than the conscious level and gives you insight into the thoughts from the surface. Your thoughts, memories, and dysfunctional feelings can be reached in this brain wave. This is where you can find your passions, intuitions, and solutions conjured by previous experiences. Creativity and wisdom hide in the preconscious state when you enter the slower brain waves.

The final state is when you dig into the heart of the subconscious mind with delta waves like you do in deep sleep. This is where your highest self lives and your reality is present. It controls your core mentally and physically. This powerful level gives you access to a collective consciousness state if you enter the delta waves through transcendental meditation or deep hypnosis. You're activating the subconscious level without shutting the conscious level down entirely. They can now communicate with each other and this is how you instruct the subconscious mind to absorb new evidence through visualization. You have conscious access to the deepest library within your mind. However, reaching the delta waves intentionally comes with a lot of practice. Settling for the alpha waves is where most people are comfortable.

Either way, our beliefs, thoughts, memories, habits, behaviors, deeply embedded emotions, and everything within our knowledge are finally reached with the intelligent mind. Meditation has successfully slowed the brain waves to reach this state where you can marry intelligence with the deeper reality inside of you (EOC Institute, n.d.). The two minds overlap and your critical thinker finally has all the resources it needs to influence the subconscious mind. The conscious mind is the part of the iceberg making requests from the lower entities after all. Consciously thinking about what you want isn't enough information for the subconscious mind. A clear communication where you paint a sensory interactive image for the subconscious is how it stores the information properly.

Remember that the subconscious mind has no access to the external world and you need to visualize experiences to help it latch onto the image you seek.

The subconscious mind automatically translates the sensory stimuli you're providing it with and stores this in memory. This loyal servant then works behind the scenes to manifest the concise instructions it receives. The conscious mind has the advantage of being our daily operating system that gathers chosen information from the environment, people, and experiences. The beauty with the conscious mind is that we can control it with our intentions and logic. This leads to automatically controlling your subconscious mind because it won't question your input.

Allow your conscious mind to translate information logically and the subconscious mind will fill in the blanks if you give it the information to do so. It can only subliminally influence you with the information it has already. The subconscious has this huge responsibility for a reason. The conscious mind's brain waves are traveling too fast to capture the millions of fragmented information we experience every second of our lives. It filters the data and sends what's necessary to the subconscious mind. Meditation allows you to control this filter so that you don't lose invaluable information either. You become aligned with your consciousness levels and this has benefits you can't imagine.

Think about the last time you did anything creative. Did you paint a picture or play an instrument? What many people don't realize is that when they enter "the zone" in their creative spurt, they're also entering the lower wavelengths. The subconscious mind contains much of our creative edge and needs to be involved when we get lost in the moment of what we love doing. We can find inspiration in this vast storage region as well. When was the last time you had to rest so that you could gather the inspiration needed to complete a task? I was faced with a situation on the ranch and my logical brain fell flat. Yes, intelligence exists in the conscious mind, but it's nothing special without creativity.

The moment I enter a peaceful state, where my waves slow down, is the moment inspiration hits me. That's why the most successful people are inventive and creative. It doesn't mean that they don't use their logical intelligence. They need intelligence to invent a creative concept or solution to a problem. The two consciousnesses need to work together for someone to be hugely successful.

Let's revert to religion for a moment. Religious people believe strongly in prayer, but little do they know that it's another form of meditation that helps you get to the subconscious level if you do it right. People pray because they desire something, or they wish to deliver hope to the creator within their minds or by following their religion.

Prayer is faith, whether it's in a God or the creative powers within your mind. The truth is that prayer won't work if you aren't clear and concise either. How can a new reality manifest if you can't visualize the result? Your God or the subconscious mind you're relying on needs to understand precisely what you want. Faith also teaches us to visualize our outcome, but we need to be patient. Religious people don't pray every day for the same thing. They ask once and will take moments to visualize their outcome and how this makes them feel. They'll become one with the result, but they won't nag their spiritual creators. Faith can also mean that we must live as though we already have something that we asked for, even though it hasn't manifested yet.

That's why you need to continue visualizing the result as though it's already genuine. Leave the subconscious mind to manifest the new design over time. It took eight years minimum to design your current reality. In fact, it took your entire life to complete the current framework. Give the creativity in your mind time to manifest your desires. Religious people can maintain their faith in their Gods to manifest their new realities. The wait can be grueling, but even the Gods didn't make the earth in the blink of an eye. As a rancher, I can confirm that the soil must be prepared before you plant the seed. The subconscious mind is the soil and the seed is the result you visualize. This seed must also be guided carefully by showing it how great the results can be when it turns into the manifested tree you want.

Marisa Peer is an expert in hypnosis, and she explains it in terms we can understand better (Buckley, 2019). The subconscious mind is also your keeper. It protects you and its ultimate directive is to steer you clear of pain, unpleasantry, and unwanted experiences. It must keep you alive as long as it possibly can. One can call it our will to survive and that's why it controls the conscious mind so robustly. The program within the subconscious is hardwired to defend you and is influenced by imagery and languages from the conscious mind's experience in later life. Understandably, the subconscious mind will retaliate against any desires in the conscious mind if these images are warped. This powerful part of you also prefers familiarity and visualizing outcomes can turn the unknown into something acceptable.

Language is also stimuli for the subconscious mind and it picks up experience through the words you speak. That's why affirmations are also useful. We speak and visualize things into reality, especially when our words are constantly dark or light. Those automated defense mechanisms will kick in again as false protection from the pain. Your partner always told you that you can't be anything but a homemaker and now you give up on your brilliant business idea. Marisa Peer has used this relationship between the consciousnesses to understand and treat the subconscious correctly. She has successfully activated the subconscious to work with the conscious mind in her patients. She developed the famous Rapid Transformational Therapy that has proven to reprogram the subconscious level.

Hypnosis is similar to meditation and it has proven to help older people remember their past clearly, even 50 years later. Peer's work proved that slowing the brain waves can give us access to photographic memory, by guiding her patients verbally and helping them paint those priceless images in their minds. She's even helped people quit smoking and change their habits when they were spiraling downwards into self-sabotaging behaviors. Learning about the activation of the subconscious mind sounds very much like using our imagination to create a picture that will help fill the blanks where logic stops in the future. The connection between the subconscious and imagination is undeniable and that's why we need to examine this further.

Chapter 3:

Imagination is the Key

Remember your childhood when the world was your oyster? I recall swinging as high as the chains could carry me, while I imagined being a space traveler about to ascend to the moon. I could feel the lift-off and the rushing wind passed my face as I hopped off the swing and touched down on the moon's surface for exploration. This is often the last time people intentionally use their imaginations synonymously with their subconscious minds. Childhood becomes more distant in the rear-view mirror, and we lose sync with the realization that imagination creates our reality. It's the key that unlocks the subconscious mind and helps us write our stories. As you imagine your future, so shall it be.

Writing Your Story

It's funny how we become afraid of using our imagination as adults because we fear the reactions of people around us. Admittedly, it would seem strange if an adult was flying to the moon on a swing set in the middle of a busy playground. Some fears aren't without good reason. We can't imagine that we're speeding down a highway in an unstoppable, untouchable, alienistic car because there are rational rules to follow when driving. That's where the conscious thinker's logic comes in handy. Our imagination as adults needs to be governed by logic, but not subjected solely to it. If logic says that you're going to crash into the barrier then I suggest you listen.

Imagination combined with rational thinking is the most incredible method of using the subconscious mind. It distinctly separates us from the remainder of the animal kingdom and makes us human. Using it in adulthood is as close to having superpowers as we'll ever come. This superpower can be seen everywhere in our reality when we compare ourselves to lesser evolved animals. Bears, pigs, and cows have never invented anything. Imagination is used to fill the void between logic and creativity. Think back a few decades. The technology was far from what we're fortunate to have today. Mobile phones were alien and so were home computers. Think back a little further. Wilbur and Orville Wright defied people's rational ideas of reality when they took to the skies in the early 20th century.

How do you think they concocted such a crazy idea? The Wright brothers allowed their imagination to give them insight into a new reality. If they didn't think of flying, and if no one else did, we would still be grounded like primitive mammals. The key here is that they didn't just think of flying, but they imagined what it would feel like to be among the birds who defy gravity. They took inspiration from birds to develop wings that soared through the air. We would never have landed on the moon if someone didn't imagine it first. We couldn't have the convenience of technology if no one cared to imagine new ways of defeating seemingly impossible feats. Primitive animal species don't have this magical blend of consciousnesses that brings the powers of genius and creativity to the same table.

The secret with adulting and imagining at the same time is to understand how influential, powerful, and fast this process becomes when we learn to use it. The fact is that you're using your superpower combination every time you plan anything. Your logical mind takes care of the facts while your imagination gets information to and from the subconscious mind. You can't plan a party without imagination because it would be pretty bland if you did. You also can't plan a vacation without having some creative ideas. These imaginary ideas are instigated by memory or sensory stimuli you received from brochures or television adverts. You also can't solve complicated problems without some influence from your imagination.

It continues to fill the blanks from your subconscious mind while you try to figure out how you can get your hands on the rarest concert tickets. It stirs when you need to plan your presentation at work when you're trying to get a promotion. Imagination quickly fills the gaps with inspirational ideas that turn somewhat impossible or adverse complications into opportunities. Every entrepreneur is an imaginative genius. It helps you answer irrational questions because you need to try something new, something crazy. Even home decorating is ignited with imagination. You wouldn't have a clue where each furniture item belongs unless you spend time imagining where it would look best. Your mind measures the space and visualizes the couch in a certain position.

Honestly, you've never stopped using your imagination when you grew up. You only hide from it because it doesn't seem intelligent now that you've evolved from your swing set chronicles. The imagination is the speedy communication between your subconscious and conscious minds. It's commonly thought to have a mind of its own. This has been a problem for many people because their lack of control over their imagination is misleading and destructive. We must regain control through conscious effort to avoid our imaginations from leading us astray and creating faulty realities. Having an unchecked "mind of its own" isn't an option for success.

We can control our conscious mind intelligently to make sure the imagination creates a reality we wish to live in. Let's understand the imagination before we learn how to use it.

Functional Influence

There's no doubt that imagination leads the way to success even before we consciously recognize what's happening. Think about any example where you behave a certain way or complete something without thinking about it. We have to imagine the journey from our desire to its outcome before we experience it, even if this happens milliseconds before we do it. Your subconscious mind is the journey, your goal is the destination, and your imagination is driving you there. Let's say that you have to sign a new client up this week. That's your logical mind telling you what's needed for success because your boss will be happy with the intended result. The outcome in this scenario is a client signing a contract. The conscious mind recognizes this and your imagination pulls the strings now.

It ignites a visual directive from the subconscious mind without thinking about it because previous experience says that you always make your clients sign. You haven't missed one yet. Your imagination uses the subconscious to automatically map the visual route to this outcome. You know how you're approaching this client within seconds. The imagination has set the stage for meeting them in a friendly coffee shop and even pushed ideas into your mind about how you'll entice them to sign the contract. You'll compliment their shirt and ask them how their kids are doing. Everyone loves being asked about their kids. This is a creative icebreaker. Your imagination is drawing this image in your mind even before you sit down with the client.

This automated response pushed into the conscious mind is what motivates you to see your plans through. The image is clear but could also be negative if you've experienced trouble with clients before. Now the imagination starts pushing all these crazy ideas into your conscious mind and you panic. Fear is a manifestation of imagination in this case. You can see yourself trembling and stuttering instead of being the confident person who needs to reach the outcome their boss instructed them to. However, this manifestation brought on by a visualized reality happened so fast that you didn't acknowledge it. The next thing you know is that you're sitting in awkward silence across from the client.

The fear has evolved into physical reactions in your body now because it influenced your conscious mind into believing that you should worry about this meeting. It doesn't matter if you've never met this person before because your subconscious mind doesn't have the information to confirm this fact. It only knows what it remembers in past failures and uses this to manifest anxiety through your imagination that turned real faster than you could stop it. This is called the law of attraction in psychology. Your imagination and conscious input will stir the subconscious mind into responding without logic controlling it. Imagination is the key to unlocking the control you need over the law of attraction (Sasson, n.d.-b).

Prentice Mulford was the creator of the concept that everything we give the world will become our reality in the 19th century. There are seven laws of attraction in his theory to be precise. The first is *the law of manifestation*. This mental law explains that everything we focus on hard and long enough will manifest in our reality. The power of the subconscious mind is in agreement when we learned about realities in chapter one. The second one is called *the law of magnetism* that indicates that our thoughts are powerful enough to attract what we want and motivate ourselves. The third is called *the law of unwavering desire*. This means that we must intentionally want the desire even when we're thinking about something else.

The fourth one is called *the law of delicate balance*. This teaches us to appreciate what we have and not become overly obsessed with our desires because we might not get exactly what we visualized at first. The fifth is called *the law of harmony*. This means that we must never forget that we're made of the same substance that everything in the environment is made of, and we can only use a harmonious balance to pursue success by tapping into our full potential. This law tells us to use controlled intelligence to regulate our imagination. The sixth is called *the law of right action* and is quite similar to Buddhist karma teachings. What you give to the world will come back, whether it's negative or positive.

The final concept is called *the law of universal influence*. This law reminds us again that our particles are of the same substance as everyone else's, and the energy resonating from it shouldn't negatively interrupt other energies. You should never use your imagination to compromise someone else because the ripple effect will come back to you according to the previous law. The truth is that every plan, ambition, desire, or goal starts as an imagined vision in the mind, and you can use the laws of attraction to empower and motivate yourself towards the goal.

The imagination has helped many successful people reach astonishing goals (Harish, 2014). Walt Disney would never have built the empire that exists without it. His amusement parks are known globally and their movies and characters are out of this world, literally. The engineers who work at the theme parks are called Imagineers for a reason. Walt Disney had a vision, and he turned it into a reality that has been enjoyed for decades now. He could never have thought of these revelations in entertainment if his imagination was stagnant. He isn't the only successful achiever among the famous either.

Michael Phelps was an Olympic swimmer who walked away with eight gold medals. His coach was amazed to see how powerful his vivid imagination was in setting new records and beating his competitors. Harish interviewed his coach, who spoke of Phelps sitting in the stands, visualizing multiple outcomes, so that his body and mind were ready for anything. He would play the outcomes in his mind like a rolling film of failures and successes in his race, and he'd then choose one outcome when he hit the water. Even when Phelps still won the race when he was the underdog, after colliding with another swimmer at the Milan 2009 world championships. He even beat someone who mocked his meditative state before the race.

The truth is that your imagination resides between your conscious and subconscious minds. It has been difficult to allocate specific regions of the brain to either imagination or automatic responses from the subconscious mind. However, what we do know is that you have an explosion of potential the moment you combine the imagination with the vivid emotions and memories in the subconscious mind. Using visualizations is the way you can communicate simpler instructions to the subconscious mind with your imagination. Motivating yourself with visualized desires is how you get through the endless filters spread throughout the brain, so that the subconscious mind can store new information.

Silencing the mind with meditation and drawing that image is the best way to convince the subconscious mind to listen to reason. Brute force isn't the way we make it follow instructions. The subconscious mind will become more active and susceptible to suggestion from your imagination when you enter a state of relaxation. Becoming part of the imagined vision is crucial because this helps the subconscious mind store the emotions from it too. You can't just close your eyes and draw a mental image. You need to feel the emotions in your vision. Never forget that your subconscious mind has no connection to the outside world. It relies on you to show it how this goal makes you feel.

Believing in the imagination is also non-negotiable. Amy Purdy is known as the highest-ranked adaptive female snowboarder in the world, but she didn't start there (Harish, 2014). She was a humble massage therapist who dreamed of traveling the world and snowboarding off the highest alps. Tragedy struck when she suddenly developed meningitis and lost her legs below the knees, a kidney, and her spleen. Purdy didn't allow this to hold her back once she mastered her imagination. She designed her own prosthetic legs and entered the world of competitive snowboarding. She won two gold medals and now appreciates the power of imagination. She consciously decided to believe that her reality will form around her imagery.

Our inner child has never died, they've simply grown older and lost touch with the imagination when the higher thinking brain developed. Things don't need to make sense at first. You need to decide whether you'll allow fear to control your imagination or whether you'll become an Imagineer instead. Remember that your imagination will conjure manifestations from your subconscious mind, whether you want this or not. Approaching this intelligently doesn't mean that you must repress the child inside of you. This gives way to the negative outcomes that adults will inevitably endure throughout their lives. You must rather awaken the child and allow your imagination to bridge the gap between the two minds.

Logic doesn't disappear at all but rather guides the imagination to assert a strong connection. Use your superpower to improve your performance and reach your goals as many people have before you. Successful people didn't get where they are by repressing their imagination. Remember to think positively, too. Why would you want any other reality?

Unlocking the Best Version of You

Imagining a future where you're happy, successful, and achieving your dreams is the most powerful motivator your intelligent mind can use to influence the subconscious mind. It's the creative power needed by inventors and the world's best party-planners. We use it when we paint, write a book, or design an excuse for why our kids can't do what they want. We need this power to build an empire as entrepreneurs. You can unlock the opportunities by using your imagination to attract what you need into your reality. The only question that remains is how we imagine our futures. Not everyone can paint an image in their minds, whereas others can immerse themselves in a fantasy that engulfs them.

We can travel anywhere we choose at the speed of light behind closed eyes, but some people struggle to awaken their inner child. The secret is a conscious effort because this is how the thinking brain controls the imagination. It's difficult to conjure images when you don't believe in the process. Some people will find it difficult to paint this image even once the child is awake, and this is okay. There's good news as long as you're making the effort. The imagination isn't limited to vision either. It involves all our senses and emotions to magnify the results. You can imagine smelling something. Can you remember your mom's famous apple pie? Imagine smelling the pie and you'll quickly realize that your emotions automatically surface from the subconscious mind.

Allow the emotions to engulf you as you imagine the taste when the cinnamon-flavored filling touches your tongue. Imagination and memories can coincide to help you practice visualizations. The idea is to open your creativity hiding in the subconscious mind with your imagination. Getting lost in memories opens the doorway between them. Think about the softest, subtlest material you've ever felt against your skin. Maybe you're a lover of silk. Imagine the silk embracing your skin gently. Feel the freedom in your memories as you recall the time you stood on the beach with the wind gently brushing your sun-kissed face. Daydreaming has been shunned upon, but it's always been the doorway that led to incredible changes in people's lives.

Children might dream of the craziest things we can imagine, but adults have the additional tool of reasoning with their images. Don't imagine things that aren't within your rational understanding either. An artist can't imagine inventing a device that makes cars run on air. Their talents lie in art and this is where they should expand. They can draw mental images of an incredible showstopper. They can also picture places they wish to travel to. However, they aren't engineers or scientists. Never forget to use your logical mind to guide your creative visualizations. You're capable of more than you think, but don't expect things that can't happen. The artist can rather envision himself studying engineering. This is not called daydreaming. This is called visualizing and creating a brighter future.

Learning to use your imagination isn't complicated. Becoming aware of it is the most profound step you can take. Find a comfortable place to sit and close your eyes for a moment. All you need to do is reflect on the newfound awareness. How does it make you feel? Can you see an image? Where is your mind going right now? Don't resist if your mind wishes to make you travel to your best memories. You want to think about how your life has been influenced by your subconscious mind before. Try to remember how your imagination has brought you out of a troublesome issue in the past. Just sit there with these thoughts for a moment; feel the emotions running through your body while you follow your memories into their hidden corners of your mind.

Come back to your chair when you feel relaxed from the memories. Now I want you to think about things you do daily that are so automatic that you've never noticed them before. Is there anything you do without thinking? Imagine the presentation you finished at work. It seemed so challenging until you were finished. Let these emotions flood you now. Feel the relief you experienced when your presentation was the talk of the office. Are there any daily rituals you don't approve of? Make sure you *want* to be doing everything you do on autopilot. You need to decide whether the negative autopiloting helps you get any closer to your goals. This is only a reflection exercise, and you can open your eyes as soon as you've recognized your current usage of the imagination key in your daily life.

There's a little secret to training yourself into creative visualization if you struggle to find your senses or feelings inside of this exercise. It will take practice, but so do all great things. Take an object like fruit or even a photograph into your chair as you sit comfortably again. Don't close your eyes yet and rather stare at the object for two minutes. Interact with the object through your senses. Size it up, smell it, look at the colors, and feel how it feels between your fingers. Close your eyes after two minutes and visualize it now. Use all the senses you used when your eyes were open. You can open your eyes for a few seconds if you feel lost in your visualization. Close them and try again. Keep doing this for 10 minutes daily until you teach your imagination to be disciplined.

Many people struggle with meditation because they aren't disciplined, or they don't believe in it. This fallacy often comes because people are impatient. It takes time to master your imagination on your terms. You might never see visual images in your mind, but you might experience them through sound, smell, or touch. Keep practicing it until you get it right. Make sure your thoughts are positive as well because you don't want your subconscious mind latching onto negative thoughts. Your intention and goal must remain stable, specific, and positive for the subconscious to understand exactly what you want.

Reflect on the complexities that exist between the conscious and subconscious minds to understand the role of each. The subconscious will always overpower the conscious mind and the way to unlock this is by turning your imagination into a leader. Lead your thoughts, emotions, and behavior to a new reality. The subconscious will always design the way you see the world around you and the only way you can control it is by managing the input through conscious intention. Only you can guide yourself into a new world, one where you're as successful as your mind chooses to be. Never be vague and always communicate effectively with the subconscious mind.

You cannot control the external environment, but you can internalize the strides you take to get there. Your imagination has no boundaries as any child will show you. Close your eyes, take a deep breath, and visualize your future with every sense and emotion. Do this every day and you'll become the master of your subconscious mind again. You'll design the future by creating something to aim for. The subconscious mind needs to know what you're aiming for. Give it the resources it needs. The imagination sounds like fiction but even science supports it. We'll look at the evidence in the next chapter.

Chapter 4:

The Neuroscience Behind It

We've established that you shouldn't jump off the edge of a cliff, like a child thinking their arms are wings. But endless possibilities are waiting for the person who uses the tool they're born with. Neuroscience brings us the answers as to why imaginations are so powerful. I didn't build my understanding of the human mind without looking through the lens of science. This chapter will provide evidence and give structured support to the claims made in the last chapter, because the imagination can control the world and the future you seek. It influences our cognitive perceptions and designs the life we dream of. Let's look at confirmatory evidence.

Microscopic Creativity

Thinking about an image seems simple enough. Our memory and cognitive functions act together to create a picture of something we've seen before, whether it comes from long-term or short-term memory. The human brain is complex but far more interesting if we look at it. Creativity is present in every person as soon as they become curious about learning in their environment. You'd easily conjure up images of things you know about. You can see a pineapple, banana, cat, dog, tree, or a ladybug as soon as you're asked about them or think of them. This process is automatic because your thought processes known as cognitive abilities work at speeds you can hardly imagine, especially if your brain is functioning on gamma waves that travel at more than 40 cycles per second.

This process became automated because of your memory storage. Your brain latched onto symbols, colors, and shapes as soon as you saw your first tree. The brain is populated by neurons that transmit information from one to the next. There are billions of these little guys and connecting them is the network of what scientists call synapses. The brain is just as complicated as the universe under the microscope. Mapping it perfectly is currently impossible and that's why we can't invent a working artificial intelligence yet. The problem is that this complicated network acts as a creative artist that pieces neurons together when we think of anything. The neurons are where memories are hiding and the synapses are like electrical currents that communicate between them. You can call these connections messengers.

The network has proven to be larger than our current technology can measure accurately. This is interesting because it proves that memories exist everywhere in the brain. The only difference is that conjuring them up will require varying efforts because some memories are further away than others. Our cognitive prowess or higher thinking is located in the prefrontal cortex, according to Neurologist Andrey Vyshedskiy (Vyshedskiy & Dunn, 2015). The neurons that contain memory are spread across the brain, including the midbrain where the limbic system resides. Neuroscientists use magnetic resonance imaging (MRIs) or functional magnetic resonance imaging (fMRI) to scan the brain and record electrical activity while stimulated or at rest.

Vyshedskiy prefers the latter kind because it watches the metabolic functions in the brain, or in simpler terms, the communications between the neurons. Regular MRIs only show the neurons and not the activity. Nevertheless, she has found amazing results to prove that our memories are stored and activated when we think about images or other sensory cues. She managed to record the activity in certain regions, connecting neurons like a web, when her epileptic test subjects were asked to look at images. She even recorded the speeds at 30 cycles per second as the communication traveled through these messengers. The subjects were asked to think about Bill Clinton or a lion when they recorded these speeds.

Interestingly, the Clinton memory activated fragments or neurons vastly spread out across the brain. These neurons communicate electrically with each other like a collage of photos coming together to make one image. The same happened with the lion activation. All the participants had been introduced to the likes of a lion and Clinton beforehand, so that their brains already stored the information in these pockets that come together to make a collage. The posterior cortex of the brain was also involved in lighting up the scanner. This is how Vyshedskiy and her team confirmed that our cognitive thoughts instigate the communications that bring these symbols and colors into a whole image.

Neuroscience successfully recorded the brain's creative ability to remember something, and the clusters that ignite together are called a neuronal ensemble. The process of activating them with stimuli is called the Hebbian Principle. Stimuli will instigate thoughts in the prefrontal cortex and these thoughts instruct the clusters to connect. Memory is pretty straightforward, even if it's not currently possible to measure every memory of language and symbol each human contains yet. Now, the imagination has also been of much interest to science, because they needed to understand how the brain can reach every collage at the same speeds to prevent unsynchronized images when someone needs to imagine something unusual.

Think about the Greek minotaur of a man with a bull's head. You've probably seen one in mythology at some point and can relate anyway. Take it another step forward now and imagine a porcupine balancing a balloon on their spikes. Chances are that you'll have trouble picturing these two seemingly common images together. That's because your memories have no storage of this image. It also makes no sense to see these images as one. You can see the porcupine or the balloon, but seeing them together is more complicated for the brain. Try the same exercise with anything. Let's use language versus objects because every neuronal ensemble contains every sensory input in a fragmented neuron.

Try imagining a picture of what you call a tree and see yourself pointing at it while calling it a bed. The images and language cues don't make sense together, which makes it harder to picture them. It's like waking up one morning and people tell you it's nighttime when the sun's shining bright. Your brain can only make sense of what it knows in memory. Combining language or verbal cues with an unfamiliar object is strenuous. Our language makes up networks of its own that connect to various ensembles. Remember a time you directed someone over the phone. You used landmarks and said that you're across the road from the house with the huge treehouse in the front yard. You even told the person to turn left and right at certain points. Some people get confused with left and right but most people's ensembles know how a left turn looks.

Vyshedskiy and her colleagues ran one more test on the epileptic subjects before sending them home. They wanted to confirm whether a theory called mental synthesis was true. This theory suggests that the cognitive power in the front of the brain is capable of adjusting the instructional speeds to activate two images simultaneously, even if the neuronal collections are far apart. She asked her participants to imagine Clinton holding the lion and was happy to find that the activation took place in both her recorded clusters for the lion and Clinton. The communications reached each cluster at the same time. This proved that her subjects managed to imagine Bill Clinton holding a lion on his lap.

She tested the theory further by adding a third cluster she had tested on her participants in the memory round. The Sydney Opera House was also recorded in the first experiment, so she asked them to imagine Clinton sitting in front of the Sydney Opera House while holding a lion. It was a success because all three memory clusters connected simultaneously. This is mind-blowing evidence, because people can imagine visualizations of things they've never seen. The only question remaining was how the cognitive instructions managed to manipulate the speeds. Now we know why the minotaur is so popular in mythology and how Satoshi Tajiri took the young world by storm with his Pokémon in 1995.

Tajiri used mental synthesis to create animal-like creatures that were inspired by genuine animals. He then took popular fiction culture and created elementary animals, such as a mouse called Pikachu that electrocutes its opponents. There was also a tortoise-like creature that blasted water cannons from its mouth called Squirtle. Tajiri continued to create these fictional creatures and combine their realities with earth, fire, and other elements. He's one of the most successful men in the world today and his creations live on 25 years later. The possibilities are endless when we use multiple clusters to form new images. However, we must first learn how to control the cognitive thoughts that work with our imagination.

Thoughtful Control

Scientific theories have confirmed that our thoughts are ignited in our higher cognitive region in the prefrontal cortex behind the forehead. Science also confirmed that our higher cognitions process information to build a memory, instigate emotions from it, and decide on a response. There's been a lot of progress in the world of neuroscience, but you must also note that it's mainly theoretical. But then again, most of science is theoretical. Scientists have all these great ideas, but unfortunately, not much in the line of definite answers. Everything starts as an idea, though. That's how we've advanced in technology, medicine, and communications. Scientists are Imagineers themselves, even if some of them won't admit it until they have more evidence.

They contain the creative edge and the intelligence to make ideas work. A scientist wouldn't exist if they didn't test obscene ideas or create useless inventions first. It's what the scientists do with the information they retrieve and how they experiment with it that matters. They also gather images in their minds and must use thoughtful imagination to piece the puzzle together. Nevertheless, science has been focusing on cognitive processes to understand the human mind better. There's an automated thinking process and this helps us reminisce on the memories we have stored. This is where these Imagineers focused first.

Comparing the automation in the brain to computers, this process is formally called the default mode network (DMN), according to research at the University of Florence in Italy (Gronchi & Giovannelli, 2018). They recorded various brain activity during resting and active stages of thought. The resting stage is where the brain is running on autopilot; this happens while we're awake. Our brain waves are functioning faster and thoughts, responses, and emotions become automatic. I'm sure this sounds familiar because it's precisely what you think it is. The DNS is simply a technical term for the subconscious mind. The interesting conclusion of their research is that the brain was active in various regions during the resting stage, but there was less activity when the brain became silent in sleep or meditation.

This is understandable when the slower waves are active and our logic is capable of penetrating the speedy highway before decisions are made spontaneously. Their research also opened the doors to answers that could help us understand how the cognitive brain can send instructions to various clusters of memory at speeds that would ensure simultaneous activation. The Dual Process Theory has been under the university's microscope. Science has known for a long time that some of us think before we speak and others act before they think, even if this is counterintuitive to our success. The theory suggests that there are two types of cognitive thinking. One is deliberate and slow, whereas the other one is automatic and swiftly associative.

Psychology has classified these thoughts as either system one or two. The first kind is the fast-acting thought that is synonymous with our automatic habits. It doesn't always contain reason and is rather intuitive or impulsive. For example, I smell cedar and my thoughts immediately stimulate my memories. Suddenly, I find myself lost in the memory of the massive cedar trees at my favorite lakeside vacation spot. I can see them in my mind, and I can feel the emotions that run through me, as I remember the day that I caught my biggest fish. Maybe I hear a moo and immediately think about the cows in the pasture. It's my intuition that associates quickly and designs an image. I can even feel the warmth in my stomach as the memory contains hints of unpasteurized milk straight from the cow.

The creamy touch on my tongue tickles my taste buds and I feel excited. This entire thought process happens faster than it can be stopped. Let's compare this to system two thinking. Let's say that I come to a crossroad and must choose a path. My higher, slower, and more intelligent thought process kicks in because I need to deliberate my choices. Memories from both paths will come to mind to help me. The left path was a nightmare because of the rain, but the right path is inconceivably longer. Nevertheless, the decision is simple once both memories are scanned intentionally. I'll take the longer route because I don't want my truck to get stuck in the mud. This doesn't mean that system one thinking is wrong either.

It will always look at your experiences and memories to swiftly give you a response. This makes it a positive feedback loop in most cases. The problem comes when we need to be creative and come up with new ideas. Then we need slower, more deliberate thinking. Our more intelligent, slower thought system can take over; the research in Italy has shown that this strengthens the communications to bring both memories to the front simultaneously instead of intuitively using the first idea. The first idea in the crossroads example would see the driver wasting even more time when he tries to get out of the mud, if he allowed his speedy thoughts to control his responses. The brain has incredible powers and you must never forget about its first rule.

The brain's responsibility is your ultimate survival. So, you've succeeded in using your imagination when you slow your thoughts down and give higher thinking the power to ignite two clusters at once. I've mentioned it a few times already. We must use imagination intelligently and not rashly. The connections between the consciousnesses are powered by imagination. We must remember that our higher cognitions control the speeds of communication when we try to figure out how our imagination works. Controlling simultaneous activations is a skill you already possess. You simply need to practice it now because the longer you do this, the better the communications between these clusters become.

Habits are formed when we force communications through certain synapses because of a wonderful chemical called myelin. The brain's predisposition to liking familiarity will kick in and strengthen these communication lines with myelin to prevent them from succumbing to the higher speeds. There can be hundreds of myelin coats surrounding the networks where communications flourish. Using your creative intelligence to exercise these networks is how you start manifesting a new reality as well. Let's say that you've used creative visualizations to envision a better career with a higher salary. The brain makes these communication lines concrete and prefers to use the stronger networks in the future.

So, you don't only have the motivation, but these new habits are forming and the subconscious mind lying beneath it all is listening to your desires now. Using mental synthesis is how we create new images we haven't seen yet. People who are new to visualizing and imagining a different future might need to start with images that are familiar until they expand their creative abilities. Conscious efforts and intelligent thinking can turn these wishes into reality because you design new habits in your brain. It will take time to fully manage your imagination because the automation in the subconscious mind and your faster thinking will interrupt you until you master them.

That's why things don't always work the way we want them to because we allow fast thinking to control our imagination. Conscious intention is only mastered through practice. Dual Process Theory also teaches us that both thought speeds can work simultaneously at crossroads. That's why we doubt ourselves. We're trying to deliberate on the adversity ahead of us and our fast-thinking brain is reminding us of previous failures. The problem is that most people aren't aware of the sneaky fast-brain while they try to solve problems. Becoming aware of both processes, and paying focused attention to them, has proven to help people stop the swift thoughts that try to disrupt their intentional thinking.

Manipulating Reality

Understanding how using these tricks to manipulate reality can be confirmed with evidence of the various corners of the brain that are activated during imagination sessions. The brain lights up like a Christmas tree when the reality is successfully manipulated, but the regions that activate are most interesting.

Alex Schlegel at the Department of Psychological and Brain Sciences at Dartmouth College, along with his associate students, studied images of the brain when mental synthesis and dual thinking were used accurately (Nordqvist, 2013). They also wanted to know how imagination was used to manipulate the imagery in our minds. Recording the activity in our brains is still rather complicated, much like studying all the stars in the sky.

The researchers asked participants in an experiment to imagine a bumblebee that has a bull's head. This sounds as crazy as the minotaur in Greek mythology; however, most people have no problem piecing this image together. The brain must construct an image from nothing though because no one has ever seen this mutilation before. Schlegel and his team thought that the participants would light up the prefrontal cortex like a city, but they were surprised to see multiple regions in the brain activate on imaging devices. This also diminishes the theory that our creative thoughts come from the right brain alone. It also trumps any ideas that logic only resides in the left prefrontal cortex. The results showed that all four hemispheres in the brain activate like fireworks.

The occipital lobe is where vision is stimulated and this also lit up. The cerebrum which houses the habitual basal ganglia and hippocampus are also activated. The posterior parietal cortex that controls our decision-making, attention, and perceptions also showed activation. So did the auditory cortex responsible for sound processing, frontal eye fields involved in visualization, and the medial frontal cortex that controls cognitive functions and emotional regulation. A total of 11 brain regions were activated during this experiment which made the researchers question their current ideas of the working brain. Using the imagination to make the conscious brain communicate smoothly with the subconscious has created imaging results that were off the charts. The visual and audio regions activations also proved that we really do have a third eye in our minds.

This explains why our realities change according to visualizations. The brain's ability to conjure images from nothing, or manipulate images from familiar ones is astounding because it means that we can alter our reality or at least the perception thereof. Imagining a sound can make you hear it according to the activation of the auditory regions. Imagining a picture with your eyes closed can even stimulate the orbital lobes that design the image in your mind. That's how imaginary visualizations are powerful enough to not only communicate clearly, but also to awaken regions in the brain that would be dormant unless we were actively daydreaming or seeing the images in front of us. It creates a hallucination of sorts.

Researchers were stumped, because they still can't pinpoint where the imagination exists. The closest evidence they have is that it distinguishes us from lesser species because it creates new communications or habits. Artists, scientists, and engineers have this connection between what can only be called the conscious and subconscious minds. Even mathematicians require creative intelligence to find formulas that work. Remember that the imagination must be the driver that gets you to your destination. The neuronal synapses in our brains correlate to the theories that suggest the mind has at least two components. We have conscious and subconscious partitions. The behavior of the imagination on these synapses indicates a subconscious nature in the neurons.

The fact that they act below our awareness is subconscious in every definition of its nature. Many of these processes in our thoughts are too fast for us to decide before we respond. Fighting against the fast-paced automation is also futile. Rather embrace the beauty of the human mind in all its extraordinary complexities and focus your attention on consciously changing the way your imagination controls synaptic behavior. This is how you truly manifest the reality you want. Use the conscious imagination to awaken and create new neurons, new habits, and new success potentials. Harnessing the power of imagination is undoubtedly the way you master the human mind.

Chapter 5:

Watch Your Inner Monologue

What would you say to a child who fell off their bike after the training wheels were just removed? Their face is a perfect blend of disappointment and pain from falling. You've made progress when you can answer this question without harming the child's well-being, emotionally or physically. That's' what you're going to learn in this chapter. Our imagination, subconscious, and conscious minds are primitively child-like, and your dialogue with them is the difference between a fantastic or dreadful reality. Our constant inner monologue is inescapable because it's the voice from our consciousness levels that help us navigate the life we want. So, let's make sure your inner voice is friendly and productive to direct you to your desires.

Tapping Into the Wrong Well

The time has come for you to harness the incredible power of your conscious mind combined with the imagination to make sure your subconscious is following suit. You have most of the knowledge you need, except for one key element that remains a mystery. You know the differences between the conscious and subconscious. You also know that you need to regain control of the thought processes that happen before they form an unwanted reality. The evidence suggests that we can use our imagination to empower ourselves and change the habits of the subconscious mind. However, visualizing a new future is futile unless you know how to control the dialogue inside of you.

The missing piece of the puzzle has already been discussed without you knowing about it. Auditory influence is just as powerful as visualizations. The temporal and parietal lobes inside the brain are responsible for capturing words and languages, while they also change your perception of them accordingly (Lee, 2017). These neurological regions must translate the meanings behind a collection of words; this stores information directly in the subconscious. Words aren't simply idle chatter because they also communicate with the internal child inside of our brains every second that we hear them. Our words are so powerful that they can even control the way we feel. Our bodies react to them and that's why we can harm the "bicycle child" with negative language after they fall.

Remember that the child represents the functions in your brain. He represents the monologue that's happening every moment of your waking life and even when you rest in delta brain waves. The brain's number one rule is to preserve the body and mind by reacting physiologically to sensory stimuli, including the inner child's voice and the external language you use. There's a tiny, but dangerous gland in the brain called the pineal gland that instructs the adrenal glands above your kidneys to respond to a threat. Negativity or poor dialogue can manifest as a false threat. The chemicals released are called adrenaline and cortisol. They're great for keeping us alert when our bodies enter the fight or flight mode.

It can stop us from doing something harmful or outright dangerous, but it can also falsely claim our mental acuity and calmness if it's released for no reason. The moment we allow our brains to perceive danger, then thoughts stimulate our fear response, and we become physiologically attached to a negative outcome. How can we expect to tackle a challenge if our thoughts are keeping us from seeing opportunities by igniting fear? We become too afraid to try again and rather give up. Our thoughts are also dialogue because the conscious brain is always communicating with the subconscious mind through our imagination.

Allowing our inner voices to become tainted with negativity, fear, and self-sabotaging thoughts is surely not the way to train our imagination to work with us. Everything has to do with our inner monologue because it's the voice of our thoughts. Saying your brain is constantly talking to itself is also not some form of madness. I'm not talking about someone who stands in the center of traffic and has conversations with the little green men floating above them. I'm talking about the voices that talk to each other in your mind and create those connections you depend on. Do you want these connections to withhold you from a great future or do you want them to push you towards it?

Remember that your brain is always striving to strengthen connections to create familiarity and this means that your negative thoughts or dialogue will paint a future you don't want. It starts forming beliefs, habits, and stronger communications that prevent you from reaching goals. The voice is inside and outside and must be controlled by you at all times. Think about your words as being an architect. The vocal architect designs a blueprint based on his knowledge. His knowledge must be based on logic and the environment to make him a conscious contender. His design must never be based on internal language unless those voices have external experience. The design he creates is our thoughts in the cognitive functions of our brain.

This acts as a blueprint from which the subconscious and imagination workers must complete their tasks. The truth is that our workers are relying on a blueprint even if our architect isn't conscious. They start building the networks of intricate systems in the mind with a blueprint that hasn't been consciously approved. Even though they're working with plans, it has not been strategically and carefully planned by a knowledgeable and experienced architect. The framework designed by the workers without proper guidance is a formula for disaster. It creates beliefs, memories, and even distortions we don't want. So, it's time to tap into this well correctly to see the reality you want by consciously controlling the inner monologue.

The human mind will be capable of countless and previously thought insurmountable actions when you start designing the blueprint that correlates to your desired future. Other than internal monologue, have you ever noticed how much better you feel when you keep telling yourself that you're feeling great? Beliefs are where our future manifests. That's why the placebo effect is so magnificent as well. Give someone candy and tell them it's a new drug that will cure their disease; watch as the mind confirms this. Scientists use placebos to "fool" experimental participants regularly. The same applies to negative effects. Do yourself a favor and choose a victim for this quick exercise. Tell that person they look as pale as a ghost. Ask them if they're okay.

Watch as they start conflicting with themselves internally because your words have convinced them that they look sick. This isn't the greatest experiment but you can tell them that you're kidding once you notice their reactions. The final obstacle that can prevent you from regaining control is when the filters in your mind have taken over. Never underestimate the power of mental filters that have been in place for eons. Psychologist Jill Weber expresses the importance of being aware of your filters (Weber, 2017). Being unaware of cognitive distortions can interrupt your progress. Cognitive distortions are when our thoughts or internal dialogue has been left to work on an undesirable blueprint for too long.

They create filters that interfere with our thoughts. There are three main types of thought disruptors that you need to reflect on so that you can stop relying on the fallacies that come from them. There is the black and white thinking fallacy that you've learned about to some extent already. It's when your thoughts warp facts and then you think that one negative experience must mean that all receding ones will be the same. You don't negotiate with your thoughts because compromising to find the middle ground isn't possible in this distortion. Emotional reasoning is the second dangerous filter. This is when you think your emotions are facts instead of seeing them for what they are. You don't feel intelligent and so this must be true.

This fallacy compromises your conscious efforts. Catastrophizing is the final filter that could harm your success. This thought thief can make you see an unpleasant future and nothing else. It prevents you from remembering the positive aspects of your life and even filters the strengths you have out of the conscious architect's view. These are the final contenders in making your journey harder than it needs to be. Allowing these filters to shape your dialogue with the subconscious is as damaging as telling the bicycle child to suck it up and stop crying. There's no compassion or confidence involved and this is needed for an architect that wants to create a new world.

The Architect's Awareness

Empowering your architect starts by creating awareness of any problems that stand between you and your desires. What thoughts have held you back before? Have your thoughts led to self-actualization or have they broken your walls down with self-sabotaging realities? There's common negative self-talk that doesn't even seem to be as harmful as it is. Let's acknowledge each of the most common examples so that you can comb through your filters more accurately. Take notes of which you use in your daily life and how they've impacted you. This will also help you see how your thoughts have mapped a reality that shouldn't exist.

The first example of believing what your words speak and how you react to the manifestation of the thoughts is one we can most relate to. Our thoughts get stuck in a rut of sorts. Have you ever thought about something you don't want happening every minute of every day and suddenly, it happens? The first responsive thought that hops into your mind is: "I knew this would happen!" Well, you're right about one thing. You knew this was coming because you were obsessed with the anticipation of it. Your thoughts have manifested a negative outcome, but the truth is that your obsession has simply helped you put too much energy into worrying about something that came true. That doesn't mean that you're suddenly psychic.

You focused so hard on the wrong outcome that you didn't do anything to change it. If you didn't obsess on how the experience would be inevitable, you'd probably have changed it. That's the problem with these negative thoughts. They prevent us from doing anything because we've already accepted the nature of what's coming. Let's say that I anticipated being scolded at work for failing to finish my presentation. My subconscious mind won't care to change this if my conscious mind accepts it. Failure to acknowledge my power to change the future has been my downfall. I was so consumed by the thoughts of failure that I never finished the presentation. If only I had spent time thinking about how to finish it instead.

Another common experience is when we have someone on our minds for a long time, and they call us out of nowhere. This seems like another psychic phenomenon between you and your friend, but that isn't the case. Your mind was consumed by thoughts of not communicating with them again, and so you never picked the phone up and called them. At some point, good friends will check in on you and that's when you think that you have this telepathic connection, but it was simply your conscious decision to do, or not to do that resulted in the call.

Another common thought we have when we face challenges is that we don't know how to do it. We don't have the information we need to accomplish what we want. For example, my inner voice says that I don't know how to play an instrument. Fair enough, you probably don't unless you've had lessons. However, the inner voice is your reality. Are you going to walk away from the instrument because you can't play it, or are you going to take lessons? The moment we rely on saying "I don't know" is the moment we fail before we begin. Your subconscious mind is only influenced by you and your imagination. The two need to work together, though. You can't imagine playing an instrument and think you'll master it this way.

You must use your imagination to motivate yourself with the incredible sounds coming from the violin, but you must consciously think about taking lessons. Don't allow self-defeating thoughts to map your inner voice permanently. You can play the most difficult instrument in the world as long as you think about learning the strings and notes. The same applies to everything you allow this damning inner voice to repeat. I don't know how to meditate is an excuse, but you won't learn if you don't allow opportunities to enter your imagination. I don't know how to solve this problem with my water heater, but I can always look for advice online.

The next mantra that resonates through your inner dialogue is rather the opposite of the previous one. It's common for people to say this is easy when they face a problem. They often say this to other people when they don't need to do it. In some cases, this is correct because a musical teacher tells his student that this is so easy a child could do it. The problem with this inner affirmation is that we also stop using our creativity when we think we've already mastered something. Let's say, for example, that I think writing is easy. I become complacent subconsciously because why do I need to improve on something I've mastered?

Don't think this way because the imagination stops looking for better, more creative options when you do. My skills and talents can always improve. Writing can improve, and so can musicians. Why would you ever want to stop improving? Would we have the amazing mini-computers we possess today if Alexander Graham Bell's telephone was the final product? Martin Cooper at Motorola decided that we need better communications than the noisy, wired phones in our homes. He saw a brighter future where we had mobile devices which later developed into the smartphones we know today. Never limit yourself because limiting beliefs are harmful.

Beliefs can also hide under the disguise of saying that things have always worked the way they have. This is conforming to tradition and accepting your past beliefs as your only options. Complacency remains dangerous and continues to prevent creativity. The negative self-talk that includes you calling yourself stupid, obsolete, unattractive, or incapable are all forms of traditional complacency. You're undermining your potential and you won't succeed by accepting lies, even if your memories confirm them. The truth is that you've never called yourself stupid. It's probably a distortion in your mind formed by teachers, employers, and parents. These words belong to someone else and shouldn't have a place in your memories. They'll never disappear but you need to convince your inner voice that someone else's words aren't as powerful as yours.

The worst self-defeating language we commonly use is when we say something is impossible. The realm of possibilities remains endless when you use your imagination. None of the amazing advancements that we have today would be here if everyone believed that things were impossible. Flying, traveling to other planets, and even radio frequencies were once impossible. Saying this will only make your inner voice confirm that you're incapable of doing what needs to be done. The imagination breaks through this fallacy because there's nothing that can't be done. Nothing within reason, of course. As mentioned, don't try to jump off a building without at least a wingsuit. Why not invent one of your own, with research and proper testing, of course?

Your thoughts and imagination are training your architect to do what's needed. These common fallacies and languages used will hurt your progress and fault your blueprint.

Designing the New Blueprint

Realizing the problems that hold you back is only the first step. It isn't enough on its own, though. Compassion is the key to making sure you don't sabotage the new design. Don't be hard on yourself for slipping up once you've learned the new language you need. Thinking about what you don't want has also proven fruitless, as you can recall from the person who never called their friend. It can also be seen in the person who waited for bad things to happen without looking for ways to change it. The subconscious collects these messages as facts and is already indifferent.

So, instead of trying to change, we simply want to create room for new thoughts and internal or external words. We aren't deleting the information stored already, but we're making space for new ones to coexist. Brute force has been advised against and that means we need to gradually and compassionately introduce the inner voice, or subconscious mind, to new ideas while it becomes familiar with them. The human mind is a powerful force, and we can't simply flip a mountain over. Gradual, positive, and encouraging shifts will help it grow in a new direction on its own.

Self-efficacy is a great word to use here. It's a skill you want to teach the subconscious mind slowly so that it can grasp the reality that you can do anything. We start by learning a new language. There are some simple rules to remember here. The first says that anything spoken by another person needs to be established as a third-person perspective. Stop your inner voice when it says "I can't do this" and respond with "you can't do this." Use the difference between the words 'I' and 'you' to teach the mind to stop sabotaging itself because of other people's opinions. Their realities aren't yours and only you can own your truth. Do this with any automated thoughts.

The subconscious says "I am stupid" and I respond by saying: "You think you're stupid, but I know better." Turn the words onto the inner voice and give other people's opinions a third-person influence. It also helps that you find the source of your inner critic that always tries to define you. Reflect on who told you this and why they said such horrid things. Was it a teacher at school who had a problem with you? What would she think today when you're a high-class executive? I bet she won't use those damning words again. Acknowledge the voice and allow it to belong to someone else. Use your conscious intelligence to prove it wrong.

Spend time thinking about how you've achieved great things daily. It doesn't matter how small they are. You can even call a friend and ask them to remind you of something you achieved. You might've repressed the memories from the time you solved a problem that no one else could. Your friends will be more likely to remember this because your confirmation bias prevents you from remembering if your subconscious has slipped into negative patterns. It's easy to think we've lost our free will when we stumble too. Your positive thoughts didn't manifest as you wanted them to, and this sends you spiraling again. Don't beat yourself up and rather look for all the amazing things that did happen. So, what if you didn't get an A on an exam. You were still the top of the class with your B plus.

You want to add three voices to your inner dialogue to change the language gradually. You need a complimenting voice who responds to every negative self-defeating thought you have. Every time you think you're not attractive enough to get the partner you want, respond to this sabotaging thought.

"You might not look like the cover of a Playboy magazine, but I have gorgeous curves and bouncy hair."

"You think you blew that opportunity, but I've got a new idea to get the client's attention with a mind-blowing video presentation."

"You think you can't have an intelligent conversation, but I know that my friends love my creative stories."

The purpose of doing this is to make sure the complimenting voice has one great thing to use as evidence against the negative voice inside. Never allow your negative self-talk to outweigh your positive comebacks. The second voice you need is the motivator. This one helps you establish evidence against feelings of being incapable or hopeless, and improves your self-efficacy.

"You think you can't get tickets to the concert, but I always win first prize when convincing my children to stop being impossible."

"You think you don't have musical talent, but I was the winner of my talent show at school."

"You assume that you don't have what it takes to negotiate peace between your colleagues, but what about the time I separated my kids when they were about to claw each other's eyes out?"

Keep motivating yourself by providing evidence of times you've succeeded in something similar. Remember that the subconscious mind represses these memories when you've been negative for a long time. Anything it thinks you can't do has possibly been done in some form in your life. The final voice you must adopt is the compassionate contender. Self-criticism is rife in people who don't act compassionately to themselves and who can't see the strengths they possess. They think they must be perfect because their mind has a fallacy where human beings are without flaws.

"You choose to be depressed because of someone else's comments, but I'm not defined by another person's opinions anymore."

"You chose anxiety when faced with adversity, but stumbling is part of learning and it allows me to grow creatively now."

"You're angry at yourself for falling off the horse, but I'm going to take riding lessons to avoid hurting myself again."

Changing your language will design the blueprint you want. You'll be fine as long as you stop making other people's voices yours and use the three additional inputs instead to soothe the subconscious mind. Our imagination will start firing in new directions when we become attuned to our inner monologue. Guiding your imagination with conscious efforts to think about your ultimate desires and not your past is the way you unfold the human mind. Now it's time to put all the advice together and form a new reality for you.

Chapter 6:

Priming the Subconscious Mind for Success

Are you ready to give your inner child the life they always dreamed of? Do you have the motivation, knowledge, intention, and desire to change the future by redesigning your daily habits? Welcome to the "meat and potatoes" of it all. This chapter will teach you how to train your brain and harness its endless power. It's time to use your imagination to create the desired reality you want. I'm going to share the tools, techniques, and daily routines that give you the edge. Knowledge is nothing without application, after all, so let's use the human mind to open your journey for success, love, and happiness.

Choosing Your Destination

Now the time has come to put all the information you've gathered to work. You have a profound new understanding of how the mind works and how it can benefit you. The first step you take is acknowledging and reflecting on where you are, what you have, what's lacking, and how the failure to apply the human mind's powers to your life has claimed victory over your desires. Be honest in your reflection and determine where your life stands right now. It's impossible to know what you want to change if you don't know what's wrong. Children can tell you they want to be a doctor or the big boss of an enterprise when they grow up, but adults have trouble recognizing what they want. That's why you need to understand what makes you unhappy first.

Think about how much time you use mindlessly navigating your daily life. How often do you plonk down on the couch and wonder where the day went? You didn't do everything you intended to do. Heck, you weren't sure what your intentions were in the first place. Take a piece of paper and record all the things in your life that exist but you aren't content with them. How much of your current reality isn't what you desire? The problem is that many people follow a default blueprint called the American dream. There's nothing wrong with this if it's the reality you want, but ask yourself whether it's everything you want, though? It's sad when people navigate life without any ambitions because they become complacent in a slow-paced dream that belongs to someone else.

Once you have your notes, you can start designing the reality you wish to see. Sit down and properly determine what you want it to look like. Remember to be highly specific because wishing to meet a romantic partner is a general goal. What do they look, smell, and sound like? You want to become an entrepreneur but what business do you have in mind? You need to know how you'll get this business, gather investors, where it's located, and why you started it. Every entrepreneur starts a business with an idea that is connected to passion. They didn't latch onto seeds that weren't within their passions. I'll only start a public relations company if I'm insanely passionate about designing presentations, managing client's reputations, and handling the heated wraps that come from bad publicity.

Are there any dormant dreams you've repressed because you didn't have faith in attracting the right resources? Why were you afraid of pursuing them? Think about whether the first step towards it would still be seemingly impossible with the new knowledge you have. The secret to designing your goals is to treat them as though they already exist. Call yourself an entrepreneur while you think about the business. You won't have much luck with investors if you introduce yourself as a wannabe entrepreneur. That's why your desires need to be specific and thoughtfully existent before you walk into a bank. Take a moment to feel the blissful emotions that wash over you as you place yourself in that boardroom.

Feel the emotions as you embrace your perfect partner. Keep in mind that setting your goals is automatically functioning as visualization. Use all five senses and your emotions to connect with it. There are seven golden rules when you envision a future you desire.

The first rule says that we must be selfish. This sounds harsh but how can you determine what your reality looks like if you're designing it for a collective group of people? You can't do this because everyone's desires are different. Never sacrifice your time or dreams for other people. Imagine yourself in a space where you aren't tied down by family, work, and friends. You need to know what this space would look like and what you'd be doing at that moment.

The second rule tells us to regret nothing. This is especially important to counter rule number one. Don't regret being selfish because you won't progress if you make everyone else's success and happiness a priority over yours.

The third rule reminds you to think about what your dreams have always told you to pursue. You must determine what matters more in your life, whether it's family, love, or career success. This rule defines your needs more than your desires.

The fourth rule says that you must be specific about what you don't want as well. It's easy to say that our job makes us cringe, but we must know why it does this. Determine whether your salary, colleagues, or employer are standing in the way of your goals.

The fifth rule counters the third one because it surpasses needs and looks at what makes you happy. Make notes of the things that make you feel like life is truly worthwhile. It could be work, children, romantic relationships, family, traveling, or financial freedom.

Which of these factors bring a warm feeling of happiness to your life?

The sixth rule is a clever one because it allows us to share motivation and success. You need to share your desires with those around you. Don't keep it a secret because your social crowd could encourage you to keep trying when you're hesitant. They can also celebrate your achievements when you reach them.

The seventh rule reminds us to never forget about the laws of attraction. We must remain positive in our desires. Every thought, verbal confirmation, emotion, and visualization must be overwhelmed with positive energy. Keep your compassionate inner voice in the spotlight if you stumble or don't achieve the precise essence of your desires.

This exercise doesn't only help you set your goals. It also starts the mindset movement you'll need on top of your knowledge about the imagination. You now have an idea of what you do and don't want. Start training your inner monologue towards helping you bring your desires to fruition once you have a clear idea of what they are. Three steps will ensure a daily routine becomes your new future. The first is when we focus intently on our desires. Conscious focus is the key to activating the imagination and creating auto-suggestions to the subconscious mind where our habits lie. That will help us establish the second step because we need a subconscious agreement to make the habits stick.

The third step is when the imagination naturally helps the process build a new reality. This three-step process will all hang in the balance of the first step. You can't get to the second or third without going through the first. The significance of the first cog in this wheel is also important to practice long enough to make sure the other cogs kick in. Only then will you have a well-oiled engine. There are multiple ways to set these steps in motion, and we'll look at each one now.

Creative Journaling

Many people shy away from journaling because it seems like something a teenager does; however, it has benefits that can't be denied. The first advantage might be the most profound. Putting our ideas on paper daily is like planting a seed before it withers. We've all had moments where brilliant ideas pop into our minds and hours later we've lost the plot. Some people have shorter memories and can forget their brilliance in minutes. The secret with journaling is to do it when your brain waves are slow in the morning or when you're relaxed. You know this is the time your brain conjures up unimaginable images without effort. Placing them on paper also helps you expand them as they're permanently recorded. The brain won't easily record memories that aren't repeated.

Remembering the idea that you had is crucial; you don't want to forget the gold when your mind enters beta waves and pushes unnecessary information out. You can also come back to it and build it into something greater. Journaling gives you accelerated manifestation, lays the groundwork for a productive day, and clarifies your goals. Your life becomes structured and erratic emotions are kept at bay. It's difficult to maintain your focus if emotions are as scattered as your daily routine. It offers stability, empowerment, and detachment from harmful emotions. Instead, you get to remember the past on your terms. Journaling doesn't only retain information but enhances your learning when you can revert at will.

It can help you expose challenges you weren't even aware of while you gain inspiration from recorded memories you forgot. You essentially become a problem-solver. Journaling also improves your gratitude which is a habit you need to obtain. Gratitude allows us to be grateful for the little things and this minimizes counterproductive experiences. Recording our daily gratitude has immense benefits physiologically, psychologically, and emotionally (Hardy, 2016). It helps you boost your health, strengthen relationships, and develop character strengths. Gratitude can enhance your career, elevate self-esteem, and improve your sleep. Other advantages include improved longevity, energy levels, romantic relationships, and goal pursuits.

Always include gratitude entries in your journaling as this pushes your mindset into the positive realm that's needed. Journaling also helps you record your history where you might see memories you can be proud of, and it unfolds your creative side. It can give your inner monologue a written voice with creative writing. Doing it every morning can even act as a self-healing form of therapy because it isn't judgmental. People tend to record their emotions and ideas honestly and end up trusting themselves better. This practice rather makes you understand how important you and your desires are, while keeping track of patterns you might be unaware of. Your intention towards goals will amplify and the power of the human mind has an outlet in your words.

Journaling offers new perspectives and helps you connect the dots if you're unsure of something. The benefits are countless, but I want you to develop the habit of journaling daily. The best way to use this technique is to apply it every morning when you wake up and your brain waves are running on alpha mode. This is when the imagination is most active. You can also enhance the experience by praying before you journal if you're religious, or you can meditate for 10 minutes. The point is to relax the mind. Even classical music can alter the waves to keep you relaxed. Remember that you're the author of your journal, so use confidence and intent to create the words you seek. Finding things to write about can also be challenging in the beginning.

Train yourself by writing about past experiences or the people around you. The beauty of journaling is that there are no rules, except for the dedication of doing it for 10 minutes every morning. End your journal with a powerful affirmation that relates to you daily. For example, "I'm going to have the best day of my life today." Now, repeat this affirmation so that your subconscious voice recognizes it. Use assertiveness and confidence until you believe your words.

Designing Your Vision Board

Vision boards are also immensely popular with successful people like Oprah Winfrey, Katy Perry, and behaviorist experts like Biologist Samuel Audifferen (Trimm, 2018). The reason a vision board is so powerful is that it gives an image to your goal. We can't achieve a goal unless we have an end in mind. Reaching it becomes the daily routine but establishing a collage of what you want shows the subconscious what needs to be done. It gives you a focus point because you must always remember the three-step process. There's no second and third cog without focus. Looking at it daily, and shaping it as you get new ideas, is how you gradually allow the subconscious mind to latch onto the new reality you want.

Think of the vision board as a canvas and you're the painter who'll create the Mona Lisa of modern days. It might not be valuable to other people, but that's why your goals are selfish. Your future might mean nothing to another person, but it means the world to you. Creating your first vision board will require inspiration from your journal, visualizations, and the goals you've set. The heaviest lifting always comes at the beginning of a task. Engineers can't just put a machine together. They need the blueprint to work from. They take time to recognize how each cog turns the next, how each belt drives another one. Start by creating your destination. The power of the vision board is most effective if it's visual.

You can use a canvas if you're artistic or you can use a whiteboard with images from magazines and the internet. You can also create one online if you visit www.canva.com. Turn the center of your board into the ultimate goal with collages of bright images. Colors and shapes also help your subconscious mind store the fragments in the neurons. The images must represent the future you desire and using bright colors also enhances memory storage. You can start working on this vision board once you have the centerpiece in place. Come back to it daily and start adding the details of the journey. Find images that represent the smaller goals you'll use to get to the larger image. These pictures must be as visually attractive as the centerpiece.

For example, the centerpiece might be your ultimate goal of how you've built an entrepreneurial empire. Use the smaller collections around it to represent the people who'll help you get there. The habits you live by can also be added. Have an image representing the required investor. Find an image of the partner that you desire because relationships make you unhappy and set you back on the centerpiece goal. Add friends, family, traveling, and even the knowledge you want to improve by studying. The only rule with your vision board is that it must resonate with your emotions. That means it must include the seven rules of goal-setting. You won't be determined or disciplined to achieve the collage of your future if it doesn't satisfy the rules.

The Power of Meditation

You must include meditation in your daily rituals as well. Newcomers could focus on 10 minutes every morning and seasoned meditators should do it at least 20 minutes daily. You can also bring your mind to silence multiple times daily. There are certain methods of meditating that enhance this technique. Sitting in the middle of a busy park is saved for professional meditators. You want absolute peace if you're a newcomer. Accurate meditation is found in using the core of focus but the human mind is like a spontaneous toddler. Meditation intensifies your focus and brings your mind to the lower brain waves you require before visualizing your desires. You'll need to practice your attention to develop discipline.

Thoughts are erratic and will disrupt you. That doesn't mean you must give up. Simply refocus your attention and try again. Many people use objects or bodily functions to guide their focus away from the external environment. You can listen to your breath pass through your nostrils if this helps you. Most meditators use breathing to relax their muscles. Other people look at an object until their mind becomes quiet.

We can also use emotions and thoughts to focus. Someone who desires love can pay attention to the way it feels. Nevertheless, it's best to enter meditation in stages. Don't focus on your goals yet. All you're doing is bringing your mind to the relaxed state it needs for the subconscious and imagination to take over. You can even practice meditation alone until you build a habit of it first.

The first step is to find a quiet place where no one will interrupt you. Sit down with your legs crossed, your spine straight, and your head raised to the heavens. You can lie down if this is more comfortable. Close your eyes or keep them open. Your comfort is the most important factor.

The second step requires you to relax. This could take five minutes but maintain your comfortable position while you slowly relax every muscle in your body. It helps to start at one point and move away from this. Start with your toes and focus on releasing any tension in them before you move onto the feet. Scan your body to see if any tension remains once you reach the temple of your head. Repeat this until you feel weightless.

The third step is to enhance your focus now, whether this is on your breath or an object you chose. You can even focus on the sensation between your body and the surface beneath you that's relaxed now. Use your senses to feel the surface that seems to not be there anymore because this can ground you. Otherwise, feel and listen to the air passing through your nostrils as you breathe. Keep doing this for another five minutes to make sure your focus is attuned.

The fourth step is where you welcome the relaxed state with affirmations. You can say your truth out loud or you can whisper it internally. This opens your heart and mind to the desire for the new truth and helps the subconscious recognize how you feel about it. Speak your truth now in any sense that relates to you. Some examples to find inspiration from are to tell yourself how you're loved and how much you love the world around you.

Become one with the emotions that follow this mantra. "I'm happy, worthy, lovable, and capable of anything." Repeat your truths until they feel real in your mind. Feel your body enter a new relaxation as you commit to speaking positive truths.

This is how you train for meditation. Move on when you're ready and add your desires to the practice.

The Essence of Creative Visualization

There's nothing more powerful in subconscious suggestion than combining meditation and creative visualization to assert your goals. Whether you believe in religion or science, the truth remains that we are either a part of God's breath or we're made of the same matter the universe holds. I'm not saying that you're Godly, but your mind's power is capable of creating new realities as you've learned through knowledge about every side of the spectrum. That's why it's time to use the creative visualization you learned about. Add this to meditation and you're certainly speaking to the subconscious mind who controls your reality. Use all your senses to speak, think, and visualize the reality you want after your mind has reached the alpha stage.

Remember the rule states that you must imagine your future as though it already exists. Be the person you want to become in your visualization and use your emotions to embody your desires. The beauty is that you won't even notice the transition when it becomes real because you've been experiencing it in your practice already. Use the power of your imagination to create the image on your vision board, the truths in your journal, and to erase the memories of what you don't want in your life. Your newfound knowledge will help you progress past the limiting beliefs in your mind. Creative visualization also comes with stages to follow to allow the meditation state to design a new reality.

Stage one requires you to decide which goal you'll focus on. I'm sure you've collected quite a few in the first exercise but use only one or two at a time when you're visualizing, especially in the beginning.

Stage two requires you to enter your meditative relaxation. You want to follow all the instructions in the previous exercise until you feel like you're melting into the surface below you. Ground yourself presently where you can enjoy the show that's about to play.

Stage three dictates that you tap into your imagination now and create a vivid image in front of you. Start with the current life you have because this is something you want to erase. Delve into your memories to create a movie in front of your eyes. Allow your senses to integrate with the image you see so that the subconscious mind knows why this reality falls short of your dreams.

Stage four is where it becomes tricky. You need to visualize yourself taking an eraser and removing this life from your mind. It won't disappear but it gives your subconscious mind some inspiration. Erase the entire image before you move on. You want to see a blank canvas where you can create a new image now.

Stage five is when you create a new place that makes you feel comfortable and happy in the deepest parts of your soul. You can use inspiration from your favorite memories to combine a mentally synthesized image. Maybe you have a favorite beach and can use this to design a combined haven where your favorite park is blended into it. Every tree you love and the bench where your fondest memories reside can be included.

I can't tell you what to imagine, but I can guide you to create a new space where you feel relaxed, loved, powerful, and use all five senses to become one with the visualization. Never forget to use all your senses and feel those emotions. Turn this into a high definition image filled with colors, feels, tastes, emotions, thoughts, and sounds. Maybe your favorite bird sat in the tree above your fondest bench. Think about the bird's chirps.

Stage six is where you bring your goals into the new image you've created. Focus on people who'll be part of your journey and the accomplishments you seek in your vision board. Be highly specific as your senses remain intact with the new image. This is where creative visualization will manifest what you desire. Maybe your goal is to find the partner of your dreams. Integrate the specifics of what you seek in them. Watch them walk onto your beach and feel the rush of emotions as they speak to you. Listen to the waves that make the perfect background for their angelic voice. Visualize yourself changing too if you desire success. Allow yourself to transform into a business person.

Stage seven is when you apply faith in your visualization. Believe that what you see already exists in your life. This might take practice but it will come with unwavering persistence.

Stage eight is used to affirm the advantages of this visualization to the people you care about and not just yourself. Being mindful doesn't mean you must forget about your loved ones in untethered selfishness. Bring two people you care about into this new world that exists. How is your future going to benefit them mutually? Imagining a future where you're successful and have a balance between home and work, could see you bring your partner and children into the vision. Watch how your children are happier because they have you around more now. Your partner doesn't need for anything anymore and also enjoys the additional time with you. Feel their emotions and listen to their laughter.

Stage nine is where you repeat your recognition that your subconscious isn't perfect. It might even be stronger than you first believed. End your sessions with a mantra that relates to what you want for the day ahead. I usually say it aloud to magnify it. I open my eyes and say: "Let this be the groundwork of possibilities for my day, but anything better is also most welcome."

That's how you use creative visualization and meditation combined to start oiling those cogs in the three steps of creating smooth realities. I'm going to give you one more priceless advantage that will help those who cannot visualize yet. Guided meditations are great for learning how to use the imagination. I've developed one that is generalized and can be customized as you start mastering it.

A Short Stroll

Imagine my voice as I guide you into a short stroll. Find your comfort and erect your head to the skies. Take a deep breath and feel the sensation as it trickles against your nose upon its exit. Take another one and follow it deeper this time. Your throat tingles as the air passes through. Keep breathing deeply until you reach your lungs. Then you can move onto your core in the stomach. Allow every breath that leaves your body to remove hints of tension in your toes and feet. Feel how the ground becomes softer, gentler, and more welcoming as your legs start relaxing too. Continue breathing like this for two minutes as the muscles in your body fall into the ground beneath you.

Take your time, however long you need, because you must be perfectly relaxed. Take two minutes, five minutes, or longer if you need it. Once you're ready, allow your imagination to come forth. Imagine yourself starring in a movie. Feel your body integrating into a vision where you're standing on a pathway. Feel the dirt under your toes and the warm sun on your face. Listen to the wind blowing gently as you concoct a taste of seawater in your mouth. This path leads to the beach where your desires live. Don't rush along the path. Look at yourself and see the shapes and colors around your body.

What clothes are you wearing? What's the color of the grass along the path? How does this image make you feel? Slowly, take a step forward and feel the emotional shift as you approach even cleaner and fresher air. Don't stop feeling the breeze and smelling the ocean. Take another step when you're ready. Don't do it until you've soaked up all the glory of the current position. There's no need to rush yourself. You can move forward and feel the essence of change as you do with every step. One step at a time, you get closer to the beach while never missing out on the full experience of where you are.

At your own pace, you arrive at the edge of the path. Now you need to design the beach of your dreams. What do you see? Is the ocean welcoming? Are the waves gentle? Is the sun teasing the horizon in beautiful shades of gold? Listen to the sounds of the waves combing over the sand. How does the sand feel here? Speak to yourself and create the beach you desire. The path behind you is gone now. You can only move towards the seashore. Allow the sand to tickle your toes and breathe deeply as you feel the joy and accomplishment of reaching the beach. Don't stop designing it either. Add more images to your beach.

Who's with you right now? Who's running along the waterline? Who's building a sandcastle? Talk to them if you want to. Tell these people how you feel. Allow them to share your imagined vision with you. Are you helping the child build the sandcastle? Are your toes wet from the water while holding hands with the person next to you? Welcome new images as you see colors and shapes change. Remain in this space, adding more to it with every breath you take. Allow this beach to become you. Give the imagination all the leeway it needs. You can stay here as long as you need to.

When you're ready to come back, you can welcome the image back with you. Tell this haven that it's okay if it manifests in your life. It's also okay if it becomes more than you imagined. Express the lack of boundaries that this vision can use when it comes back with you. Once you're fully immersed and feel the need to return, you can slowly come back. Allow the vision to become more distant as you come back to where you grounded yourself on the surface beneath you. Feel the surface getting harder again and how your body starts separating from it.

Each muscle is slowly separating from the ground now. Keep breathing as you open your eyes and just sit there, feeling the emotions you experienced on the beach. Your muscles gain weight again as you know that this day will be your greatest.

I hope you enjoyed that visualization as much as I did when I created it. Even in my words, I can carry myself there and you'll master it as such with practice. You'll find your vision even with your eyes wide open when you spend enough time in meditation. Now you know what's needed daily in your life. Make your reality your own with new routines and simple, powerful suggestions.

Conclusion

Who knew that the world was at your fingertips once you brought two minds into harmonious perfection? Many people don't know it because they watch as others reach goals, establish dreamy lives, and comb through negative events like a hot knife slicing through butter. We all looked at these people at some stage and wondered how they became who they were. It was a hard pill to swallow when we compared our realities to their lives.

We always watched people face adversity and overcome it without blinking. We wanted to know how others have mastered the human mind when it's such a beautiful blend of complexities. How did someone combine the conscious and subconscious minds to create the future they desired? It's normal to feel reluctant and think that luck had a hand in the pot; however, you know that this isn't true now.

Luck has nothing to do with who we become, how we live, and how our success blows up in a way we couldn't only imagine before. That's the secret because our imagination has connected the two minds so that nothing can stand in our way again. Life has always been filled with the doers and thinkers.

Who knew that they could be the same person? I suppose everyone thought Thomas Edison was insane or childlike. Those people were quickly proven wrong when he did the unthinkable. His imagination lit a light bulb for the first time. Everyone thought Hedy Lamar lost his marbles when he wanted to create a radio guidance system, but the response was eerily silent when he did it. We can't forget amazing people like Tim Berners-Lee for inventing the World Wide Web. Okay, it wasn't available to the general public at first, but what a creation!

I never would've mastered my mind if the internet, with its bountiful medical journals and history facts didn't exist. One man's creativity sparked the world's potential. None of these great success stories would've been possible if the impossible wasn't imagined first. The imagination is vastly powerful and helps us control the sparring consciousnesses if we know how to do this.

Fortunately, public access was given to scientific journals, philosophy, and history to confirm religion, quantum physics, and psychology. I compiled this exploration of the human mind so that you can reach the success of anyone you wish to. We've learned about the theories that confirm what reality is and compared it to ancient concepts that show undeniable similarities. It doesn't matter if you believe in science or spirituality when so many facts concur between the two.

Changing your future was impossible when your reality was once thought to be static. This is, fortunately, anything but the truth. You understand enough about the brain to see how conscious and subconscious factors work to create something we once thought was unchangeable. There might be a lot of confusion after you've studied other books that failed to cover every aspect of it.

Now, you know that using the imagination in skilled practices that have been around for as long as recorded time itself is the answer. We're all born as creative creatures and that's why we've evolved from the primitive beings we once were. We have a superpower to use in any situation to get our desires that have previously slipped out of our grasp. You're aware of all the functions that have even been recorded on medical imaging devices.

Indeed, you're the author of your story and no one can change that. Other people and the environment have nothing more than what you can offer yourself. You can internalize the instructions to make the environment work for you. You can be wealthy, happy, healthy, and as family-orientated as you want to be. The exercises were designed by people who studied the complexities of the mind and the universe.

This isn't always easy for people to do, but I dedicated two decades of my life to establish my understanding of the human mind to a point where I could use it as my armor, strength, tool, weapon, and truth. Now, you can do this too because the techniques, exercises, and new habits in this book will give you everything you need to reach your goals.

Control the voice inside of you that paints pictures in the world. Attract the positive life you deserve just as much as the next person. You can be the next Bill Gates, Walt Disney, or even Oprah Winfrey. Nothing is stopping you from using your daily exercises to get love, romance, and spunk into your life now. There's also certainly no reason why you can't combine realities as many others have.

Your mind is ready for the future, as long as you follow the golden rules of using it. The subconscious mind is the canvas, the imagination is the paintbrush, and you're the final piece that uses intelligent intentions to create the most priceless piece you can imagine. Don't let anything hold you back anymore. You have all that you need once you regain the power of the human mind.

Remember to resonate with success and don't keep it to yourself. Feel free to leave an honest review so that others can find their potential as well. Look out for my other books about understanding the human mind so that you can expand your knowledge even further. As mentioned, I have so much information piling up in my mind that I must record and share it.

My final advice to you is that you always use your mind to traverse every choice you have in life. Some will come out of nowhere, but you can control any that do. Don't allow anything to stand between you and your desires again.

References

Ananthaswamy, A. (2018, September 3). *What does Quantum Theory actually tell us about reality?* Scientific American Blog Network. https://blogs.scientificamerican.com/observations/what-does-quantum-theory-actually-tell-us-about-reality/

Andras, S. (2013, December 10). *7 ways to find out what you really want in life.* Lifehack. https://www.lifehack.org/articles/communication/7-ways-find-out-what-you-really-want-life.html

Bartleby Research. (2020). *Essay about Aristotle and Plato's views on reality | Bartleby.* Bartleby. https://www.bartleby.com/essay/Aristotle-and-Platos-Views-on-Reality-PK7GFXYTJ#:~:text=Even%20though%20Aristotle%20termed%20reality

Bergland, C. (2013, September 17). *The "right brain" is not the only source of creativity.* Psychology Today. https://www.psychologytoday.com/us/blog/the-athletes-way/201309/the-right-brain-is-not-the-only-source-creativity#:~:text=Human%20imagination%20does%20not%20come

Buckley, L. (2019, June 6). *The differences between your conscious and subconscious mind | Marisa Peer.* Marisa Peer. https://marisapeer.com/the-differences-between-your-conscious-and-subconscious-mind/

Center for Peace and Spirituality International. (n.d.-a). *What is the reality of life according to Islam? | CPS International.* CPS Global. https://www.cpsglobal.org/content/what-reality-life-according-islam

Clarey, C. (2014, February 22). *Olympians use imagery as mental training.* The New York Times. https://www.nytimes.com/2014/02/23/sports/olympics/olympians-use-imagery-as-mental-training.html

EOC Institute. (n.d.-b). *Chart: How meditation unleashes your subconscious mind power – EOC Institute.* EOC Institute. https://eocinstitute.org/meditation/how-to-harness-your-subconscious-mind-power/

Fortune Magazine. (1994, August 22). *Einstein's Search & the Illusion of Reality.* Sol.Com.Au. https://www.sol.com.au/kor/11_01.htm

Ghallagher, V. (2018). *7 laws of attraction.* Hyp Talk. https://www.hyptalk.com/7-laws-of-attraction

Glattfelder, J. B. (2019). Ontological enigmas: What is the true nature of reality? *Information—*

Consciousness—Reality, 345–394. https://doi.org/10.1007/978-3-030-03633-1_10

Gronchi, G., & Giovannelli, F. (2018). Dual Process Theory of thought and default mode network: A Possible Neural Foundation of Fast Thinking. *Frontiers in Psychology*, 9. https://doi.org/10.3389/fpsyg.2018.01237

Hanh, T. N. (2009, June 21). *Dharma Talk: The Buddhist Understanding of Reality*. The Mindfulness Bell. https://www.mindfulnessbell.org/archive/2015/01/dharma-talk-the-buddhist-understanding-of-reality-2

Hardy, B. P. (2016, October 21). *28 ways keeping a daily journal could change your life*. Success. https://www.success.com/28-ways-keeping-a-daily-journal-could-change-your-life/

Harish, H. (2014, January 27). *7 Steps to unleashing your imagination!* Launch Your Genius. http://launchyourgenius.com/2014/01/26/7-steps-unleashing-imagination/

Kaplan, D. (2017, April 30). *Meditation for manifesting your dreams - and accomplishing your goals*. Forbes. https://www.forbes.com/sites/dinakaplan/2017/04/30/meditation-for-manifesting-your-dreams-and-accomplishing-your-goals/#3ead62b636c2

Law of Attraction Library. (n.d.-c). *Using meditation for manifestation – The Law Of Attraction Library*. The Law of Attraction Organization. https://thelawofattraction.org/using-meditation-for-manifestation/

Lee, B. (2017, July 31). *Turn off these 6 dangerous inner dialogues that kills your brain power*. Lifehack. https://www.lifehack.org/618631/turn-off-these-6-dangerous-inner-dialogues-that-kills-your-brain-power

Mindvalley, & Lakhiani, V. (2016). *The power of creative visualization | Vishen Lakhiani*. YouTube https://www.youtube.com/watch?v=0mDrJtYB7zc

Nordqvist, C. (2013, September 22). *Imagination - how and where does it occur in the brain?* Medical News Today. https://www.medicalnewstoday.com/articles/266426

Operation Meditation. (n.d.-d). *Understanding the conscious vs subconscious mind in 4 steps - operation meditation*. Operation Meditation. https://operationmeditation.com/discover/understanding-the-conscious-vs-subconscious-mind-in-4-steps/

Pigliucci, M. (2020, April 24). *Stoic ontology 101: the difference between reality and existence*. Medium. https://medium.com/stoicism-philosophy-as-away-of-life/stoic-ontology-101-the-difference-between-reality-and-existence-a372f683c9c3

Plato (430-347 B.C.). (2020). Drexel.Edu. http://www.pages.drexel.edu/~cp28/plato.htm#:~:text=Plato%20believed%20that%20true%20reality

Riddle, C. (2019, July 18). *Imagination is the key to everything! | ANS Nuclear Cafe.* ANS Nuclear Cafe. http://ansnuclearcafe.org/2019/07/18/imagination-is-the-key-to-everything/#sthash.erv99zyd.7LZONA0H.dpbs

Sasson, R. (n.d.-a). *Creative visualization - attracting success with mind power.* Success Consciousness. https://www.successconsciousness.com/blog/creative-visualization/creative-visualization/

Sasson, R. (n.d.-b). *The power of imagination.* Success Consciousness. https://www.successconsciousness.com/blog/concentration-mind-power/power-of-imagination/

Sasson, R. (n.d.-c). *Your imagination is your key to success.* Success Consciousness. https://www.successconsciousness.com/blog/creative-visualization/imagination-is-your-key-to-success/

Sfondrini, A. (2018). *String Theory explained – what is the true nature of reality?* YouTube. https://www.youtube.com/watch?v=Da-2h2B4faU&vl=en

Slade, S. (2017, December 23). *How journaling is important to success.* CNBC. https://www.cnbc.com/2017/12/21/how-journaling-is-important-to-success.html#:~:text=1

Strauss, J. D. (2020). *The Christian-Biblical understanding of reality.* World View Eyes. http://www.worldvieweyes.org/resources/Strauss/Strauss-Bib-Reality.htm

The Subconscious Mind. (2018, January 4). *Your gateway to the universal consciousness.* The Subconscious Mind. http://thesubconsciousmind.com/how-to-program-the-mind-with-prayer/

Trimm, C. (2018, July 12). *Why a vision board just might be your secret to success.* Thrive Global. https://thriveglobal.com/stories/why-a-vision-board-just-might-be-your-secret-to-success/#:~:text=A%20vision%20board%20will%20help

Ultimate reality and divine beings. (n.d.). Patheos. https://www.patheos.com/library/hinduism/beliefs/ultimate-reality-and-divine-beings

van Rensburg, M. (2017, March 18). *A child's subconscious mind: How parents can hurt or help their kids.* Medianet. https://www.medianet.com.au/releases/12834 3/#:~:text=This%20trance%2Dlike%20state% 20allows

Vavra, K., Janjic-Watrich, V., Loerke, K., Phillips, L., Norris, S., & Macnab, J. (2011). Visualization in science education. *ASEJ,* 41(1). https://sites.ualberta.ca/~lphillip/documents/a sej-22-30.pdf

Vyshedskiy, A. (2016). *The neuroscience of imagination - Andrey Vyshedskiy.* YouTube. https://www.youtube.com/watch?v=e7uXAlX dTe4

Vyshedskiy, A., & Dunn, R. (2015). Mental synthesis involves the synchronization of independent neuronal ensembles. *Research Ideas and Outcomes,* 1, e7642. https://doi.org/10.3897/rio.1.e7642

Weber, J. P. (2017, July 14). *The power of your internal dialogue.* Psychology Today. https://www.psychologytoday.com/us/blog/h aving-sex-wanting-intimacy/201707/the-power-your-internal-dialogue

Wikipedia Contributors. (2019, May 29). *Reality.* Wikipedia. https://en.wikipedia.org/wiki/Reality

Williams, A. (2015, July 8). *8 Successful people who use the power of visualization*. Mind Body Green. https://www.mindbodygreen.com/0-20630/8-successful-people-who-use-the-power-of-visualization.html

Zodiac Psychics. (n.d.-e). *Your inner voice is powerful*. Zodiac Psychics. https://www.zodiacpsychics.com/article/your-inner-voice-is-powerful.html

www.ingramcontent.com/pod-product-compliance
Lightning Source LLC
Chambersburg PA
CBHW020258030426
42336CB00010B/831